How to Succeed at Work

The Ultimate Guide

By Terry Melaugh

Disclaimer

This is an information guide. It is not intended as a substitute for legal or other professional services. While every effort has been made to make this guide accurate, it may contain typographical or content errors. The information expressed herein is the opinion of the author. The author and publisher shall have no responsibility or liability with respect to any loss or damaged caused, or alleged to be caused, by the information or the application of the information contained in this guide.

Also by Terry Melaugh

<u>Get That Job - The Ultimate Guide</u>

<u>http://amzn.com/B00BV74E4E</u>

Leadership - The Ultimate Guide

http://www.amazon.co.uk/dp/B00CMR0VAI

Introduction

Introduction

The secret to success at work

This book will show you how to manage your time more effectively. You will learn how to achieve more in the limited time available. You will become more productive. You will be shown how to focus on the important issues. You will discover how to set goals and work towards them. You will learn to manage your activities, so that everything you do contributes towards your long term goals. You will learn how to progress in your career by being more productive than everyone else around you. You will learn how to gain the promotion you seek.

The secret to being successful at work is to achieve more than what was expected of you. This book will outline exactly how you should go about doing just that. By employing the techniques in this book you will surpass all expectations, particularly those of your immediate boss. You will learn how to employ a number of techniques. You will understand first of all what is holding you back. You will know what is preventing you from reaching your potential. You will learn how to set long term goals and translate these into short term objectives. You will know which tasks to carry out and which to drop or to delegate. You will understand how to prioritise your work. You will learn how to use your time effectively to get more done at work.

You will learn how to overcome setbacks and stay on track. You will know how to get the most out of your team. You will learn how to delegate your work effectively. You will understand how to communicate with and influence people. You will know how to conduct meetings. You will know how to recognise and handle stress. You will learn the importance of major project management. Finally you will learn how to aim for and get the promotion you deserve.

Doing the right things

The secret to success is doing the right things, at the right time, all of the time. The right things are those tasks that move you closer to your goals. The right time might be the required deadline for the project, or when you feel most productive. You will learn to do this all of the time, by being consistent in how you behave. The secret is to develop the right habits to help maintain momentum.

Time is a limited resource

Time is a finite resource. Time is precious. You must value your time. You must understand how to get the most from it. This is what will set you apart from the competition. No one can increase the number of hours in a day. Once the time is gone you can never get it back. All you can hope to do is to be more productive with the time and resources that are available to you.

This book will show you how to use your time to get more done than anyone around you. It will show you how to exceed the expectations of others.

Everyone has the same amount of time

Everyone has the same 24 hours available to them each day. Not everyone utilises the time to their advantage. Some people get a lot more out of their available time than others. They meet their goals and are productive. They progress through their careers and end up in senior positions of responsibility.

Other people achieve very little with their day. They often end it in frustration, with the feeling that they have achieved little or nothing. They get stuck in a rut. They stagnate. They remain at the same level. They fail to get noticed or promoted.

Advantages of managing your time

Effective time management can:

- Simplify your life.

- Reduce stress levels.
- Increase your effectiveness.
- Increase your efficiency.
- Increase your job satisfaction.
- Increase your team's productivity.
- Improve your work-life balance.
- Help further your career.

Chapter 1. Begin with yourself

Take a look in the mirror

Do you know who has been holding you back all of your life?
Take a good look in the mirror. We are usually the number one
obstacle to our own progress. We are our own greatest critic. No
one doubts our ability more than we do ourselves.

Others will have had some input in restricting your growth.
Circumstances may not always have been conducive to progress.
However the main person holding you back will have been
yourself.

The limiting factor up to now will have been a lack of self-belief.
So what you must do is to learn to believe in your abilities.

The problem with belief

The problem with belief is that it can be a positive or a negative
conviction. Belief is seldom based on facts. People develop
negative, self-limiting beliefs throughout their lives. They then
look for information that will reinforce these misconceptions.
They disregard any conflicting information that could help steer
them back in the right direction. They become trapped by their
limiting beliefs. They are restricted by the habits that they have
developed to sustain these beliefs.

Believe in more

If belief is the limiting factor, then the solution is obvious and
simple. Believe in more!

If you want to treble your salary, then the only way to do this is to
believe that you can. If you don't believe it, you won't achieve it.
If you must think, then think big.

Many people expend a lot of energy in improving skills and broadening their experience. This is commendable, but will not guarantee success.

The first step on the road to success is to increase the level of your beliefs.

Your potential exceeds your beliefs

There are no limits to your potential. Your potential always exceeds your beliefs. In order to achieve more you must first increase the size of your beliefs. Expand the boundaries of your beliefs if you want to approach your potential. When you expand the boundaries of your beliefs you will begin to grow and develop as a person.

What's holding you back?

We all hold ourselves back for different reasons. The main constraints that hold us back are:

- Not having an overall goal in life.
- Not setting priorities.
- Lacking self-motivation.
- Lacking self-discipline.
- Lacking will power.
- Lacking determination.
- Lacking self-confidence.
- Lacking guidance and a role model.
- The fear of success.
- The time we waste.
- The limits we set.
- Not being proactive.
- Letting others dictate our agenda.
- The company we keep.

Understand what is holding you back. It may be more than one of the above factors. Knowing yourself is the key to success. Recognise the obstacles you have placed in your own way. This is the first step to freeing the chains that bind you.

Identify areas of dissatisfaction

Take a close look at your career. Look at your work-life balance. Consider your relationships at work. Now identify the areas of dissatisfaction. What concerns you? What needs to be improved? What must you change?

Identify priorities for change

Having identified what needs to change, you must understand the steps required to bring about the desired results. Then look at prioritising the required action.

Identify your strengths and weaknesses

Take a piece of paper. Write down your strengths. Now write down your weaknesses. Keep the list and add to it over the next few days. You will need to work on your weaknesses. Equally important, you must leverage your strengths. To be successful at work you must concentrate on your strengths while improving your weaknesses.

Be prepared to change

Be prepared to change. Be prepared to become a new person. Start to behave as if you are the person you want to be. It will help dispel negative beliefs. To change your future, begin by changing your beliefs and your attitude. If you do this, life as you know it, will never be the same again.

Implementing change

Before you can change your behaviour, you must first of all want to change. Recognise where you are, where you want to go and how you plan to get there. Understand why you want to change.

In order to change you must be dissatisfied with your current situation. You must be able to envisage the gains. These gains must outweigh the cost involved. This is why you must aim high. If the gains are not greater than the cost, then you will not be motivated to proceed. Even if you do begin, you will give up long before you achieve your goals. You will lack the will power to maintain the required momentum.

Have a development plan

List the areas you would like to improve. Develop a plan to bring about this self-improvement. Review this plan regularly. Work on rectifying your negative characteristics.

Observe the behaviour of others

Study how others behave at work and elsewhere. Look at how people interact with each other. Notice what behaviour gets results. Notice what type of behaviour leads to dissent and conflict. Emulate the behaviour that yields the best results.

Develop your skill base

You should develop your skill base regularly. Attend courses. Read self-help books. Aim to acquire at least one new skill every quarter. If you want to reach your goals, you must improve your skills.

Adapt a life-time learning philosophy

Continue to learn from your experiences. You should strive to learn something new every day. Learn from every interaction. Ask questions. Seek to gain knowledge. Consider how well you listened to each person you met. What did you detect in their behaviour? Did you empathise with their concerns? Did you build rapport?

Do not worry about things you cannot change

There is an important category that you cannot change. You cannot change the past. It has already happened. It is over and done. You cannot go back. Do not dwell on your past. Do not let it rob you of your time or your energy. Close the door on the past. The best you can do is to learn from the experience.

Never, ever, worry about something you cannot change. You cannot save time you have already spent. You can only begin your journey from your current location.

Aim high

Aim high. It is better to aim high and miss, than to aim low and hit.

Confide in your friends

Confide in your close friends. They will often provide the confidence you need. Listen to the encouragement of others. They often have a more realistic perception of your abilities. They can give objective advice. Learn to cast off self-limiting doubts.

Chapter 2. Set Goals for yourself

Set personal and professional goals

You must set personal and professional goals if you are to progress at work. Goals provide a clear vision. Goals provide you with a destination. If you know your destination, it is much easier to manage your priorities, time, and resources in order to get there. Goals help you distinguish between important tasks and distractions.

Why Set Goals?

The people who succeed in life are those who set and keep personal goals. Winning athletes, successful business people and other high flyers all set personal goals. Setting goals provides long term vision and strategy. It also fosters short term motivation.

People with goals think ahead. They strive to achieve the significant. They know what they want. They have worked out how to get what they want. They are better at evaluating what action they need to take. They can see which tasks will move them towards their chosen destination.

Over 90% of the people who set goals achieve all or most of their objectives.

The benefit of setting goals

By creating and meeting goals you will:

- Know your destination.
- Learn to stay on track.
- Achieve more.
- Acquire intrinsic motivation.
- Increase your level of control.
- Increase self-confidence.

- Focus your mind.
- Eliminate bad habits.
- Reduce stress and anxiety.
- Increase contentment.

Growing from strength to strength

The great thing about goal setting is that, once you hit the first target, you will be motivated to achieve more. You should set progressively more challenging goals. With each intermediate target you hit, you will gain more confidence and self-belief. You will expand your boundaries. You will be able to set your sights on bigger targets. You will achieve more than you ever thought possible.

Which goals do you want to achieve?

First consider which goals you want to achieve:

- What makes you happy?
- Where do you want to go?
- What activities do you most enjoy?
- How do you want to develop as a person?
- What do you want to be?
- What do you want to do?
- What do you want to have?
- What do you want to give?
- How do you want others to view you?
- What legacy would you like to leave?

Why do you want to achieve your goals?

Next consider why you want to achieve these goals. The reasons might be intellectual or emotional. Common reasons might include:

- To earn more money.
- To save more money.
- To gain recognition.

- To be happy.
- To be contented.
- To gain promotion.
- To increase knowledge.
- To acquire power.
- To be able to retire early.
- To be able to set up your own business.
- To be able to afford that holiday.

Unless you have a definite reason, you will give up long before you ever achieve your goals.

Without goals, what are we?

If we do not know where we want to go, then how can we ever get there?

Without goals we lack vision. Without vision we lack direction. Without direction we cannot stay focused. Without focus we cannot prioritise. Without priorities we cannot make progress. Without progress, we cannot grow. Without growth, we cannot develop. Without development we stagnate.

Without goals we become complacent. We leave the outcome to chance. We drift through life without purpose. There is no sense of personal satisfaction. We become victims. We work to other people's priorities. We become followers. Our fate rests on the whims of others.

Without goals we focus on what we don't want. We concentrate on our problems and worries. We look to apportion blame for our current circumstances.

The path of least resistance

Without goals we follow the path of least resistance. We are like water that wants to flow downhill. We go with the flow. We are dragged along by an invisible force. We have no control over our destiny.

Why most people do not set goals

Most people do not set personal goals for themselves. They have not learned how to do this. They have not been shown the value of setting personal goals. They have not been encouraged to think about their own goals, aspirations, strengths and weaknesses. The need for setting goals has not been covered in their upbringing or education.

At school we have all been taught about historical and famous people and their achievements. Yet we are seldom coached in how to replicate their behaviour and achieve similar results.

How to set goals

Your goals should be specific and clearly defined. They should be realistic and achievable.

Begin by assessing your present situation. Then decide what you want to achieve. Create a mental picture of your desired results. Envisage what you want to achieve. Consider what a successful life would look like to you. Imagine the outcome and the benefits.

Write down your own personal goals. Write down the reasons why you want to achieve them. Write down the benefits that will accrue from achieving these goals. Now write down intermittent targets. Think about the activities required to meet these intermediate targets. Jot down these activities also.

Work smarter

The secret to success is not to work harder. Working harder certainly helps, but the real secret is to work smarter.

Goal setting tips

Goals should be SMART:

- Specific, in that they are clearly defined and precise.
- Measurable, in that they are quantifiable.
- Attainable, in terms that they are realistic, given the resources and talent available.
- Relevant, in that they form a clear part of your overall objectives.
- Time-bound, in that you set a target date.

Guidelines for goal setting

- State each goal as a positive statement.
- Make your goals precise by specifying target dates and amounts.
- Write down your goals.
- Break larger tasks down into smaller, incremental, more achievable targets.
- Prioritise your individual goals.
- Set goals that are within your control.
- Set realistic targets, with a degree of stretch.
- Look after your own interests.

Define your dream

Have a purpose to your life. Begin by setting your long term goals. Align these goals with your personal values. Think about the type of person you want to be. What do you want to achieve in your life? You can achieve anything you want. There is no limit. If you believe in your ability, and you have the will to persevere, then nothing can hold you back. You are in sole control of your own destiny.

Your goals should excite you. They should inspire you. You should be passionate about your goals. Your life goals should challenge you to grow and develop as a person.

Lifetime goals provide an overall perspective. They set the direction in which you want to travel. These goals will cover broad areas such as career, finance, education, relationships, family, self-development and personal well being. For each of these categories, establish your long term goals. What is your ultimate goal? Now think about where you want to be in ten years time. Having done this you can establish a plan that will help you achieve this intermittent goal.

In this book we will concentrate on your career goals. However, many of the lessons can be applied to goals in other areas of your life.

Set your own goals for yourself

Make sure that you only set goals that you personally want to achieve. Follow your inner compass. Find your true north. Follow your heartfelt desires. Listen to your inner passions. You have a purpose in life. You just need to discover it. Think about what matters to you. Concentrate on your essential values.

Do not set goals that are based on what your parents or family want you to achieve. Of course you will want to discuss and share your long term goals with your family and spouse. However, if you want to achieve your goals, you must be fully committed to them. You must have a genuine desire to succeed. You must have ownership of your goals. You must be genuinely interested in the outcome. You must be true to yourself.

Believe in your goals

You must first believe in your goals if you want to achieve them. Belief engages both your conscious and unconscious mind. It enables you to concentrate on the activity required to achieve your goals.

Do not let others limit your ambitions

Do not let others set a limit on your goals. Do not let your teachers or parents set a limit on what you can achieve. Do not conform to criticism. Do not be told your worth.

Do not let your peers hold you back. You do not need to conform to group pressures. Look at the company you keep. If it is not beneficial to your well being, you should consider changing it.

Do not set limits on what you can achieve

Allow yourself to succeed. Do not set limits on what you can achieve. Do not let self-doubt or fear stand in your way. Believe in yourself.

From childhood onwards parents and other adults influence our self-belief. If we are told often enough that we are stupid, we will come to accept this. We internalise the standards and beliefs we receive from others. This sets conceived limits on our abilities. It erodes our confidence. It becomes an obstacle to progress.

Do not foster negative thoughts and beliefs in your own ability. You can achieve anything you want. You just need to believe in yourself. There are no limits, other than those that we choose to impose on ourselves.

Keep your ultimate goals secret

If others are holding you back, consider keeping your ultimate goals to yourself. Ignore cynics and critics. Do not let others pour scorn on your goals. Keep your dreams and visions to yourself. Others at work will have conflicting goals. You will be seen as belonging to a different camp.

You may, for instance, be planning to leave in three years time to get more experience or start up your own business. It would be completely detrimental to your progress to divulge that information now. Keep your council and follow your own path.

Personal mission statement

Once you have set your overall life time goals, you should summarise them in a personal mission statement. Your mission statement should focus on what you want to be and what you want to do. It should reflect your values and principles.

Have your personal mission statement framed and hung in your home. Alternatively keep it in your diary. Use your mission statement as a source of inspiration when you are faced with setbacks and disappointments.

Long term career goals

Specify your long term career goals. What is your ultimate target? Perhaps you want to run your own business? Maybe you want to become a company director? Now establish where you want to be in ten years time. Perhaps you want to be the production manager with your current employer. This could be three steps above your current level within the company.

Medium term career goals

Having established your goals for the next ten years, break them down to a series of intermittent steps. These are your milestones. They are the smaller targets that you must hit along the way.

In order to become production manager perhaps you must first be promoted to production supervisor and then department manager. These are your milestones. Now identify the tasks that you must complete in order to reach these milestones.

You might set a target of three years to become production supervisor. To achieve this medium term goal you need to obtain additional training, extra qualifications and more experience. Each of these tasks will then become individual targets. These individual targets can be subdivided again into further detailed steps. Your training can be broken down to areas such as supervision of staff, quality assurance, health and safety, presentation skills, first aid and team building. Set a time line to achieve each of these individual goals. All of your future actions at work should be geared towards achieving these goals.

Short term career goals

Against each of your sub goals you can begin to set dates and time-lines. You should keep your long term goals to yourself. You may need to get permission for the necessary training one step at a time, without revealing your hand to your immediate boss and colleagues. You may be constrained by available budgets and the need to ensure that other people are given an equal chance. However there are external qualifications that you can achieve on your own spare time.

Once you have clear goals in mind, you can systematically go about achieving these. You will have a target for the next ten years, broken down to a yearly plan. Each year will contain definite targets that you want to hit. By reaching these targets you will begin to set yourself apart from the pack. You will be noticed as a high achiever. Your potential will be recognised. You will progress towards your goals.

Having established medium and short term targets, you will understand which daily tasks can help you move towards these goals. You can then prioritise these tasks. You will also recognise tasks that do not contribute to your goals. You can then decide to ignore, delegate or remove these tasks as appropriate.

Find the path

Recognise the path that you need to follow to achieve your goals. What is preventing you from achieving them right now? Usually you need more:

- Skills, knowledge or experience.
- Qualifications.
- Training.
- Contacts.
- Resources.

Plan to overcome obstacles by gaining the additional competencies that you require. Let your plans for the future drive your present actions.

Follow the path

Once you have established the right path, the obvious thing to do is follow that path. You will stray from time to time, but the important thing to do is to always return to the right path. Focus on your goals. Keep your ultimate destination in mind and stick to your chosen path. It will lead you to your dreams.

Chapter 3. Set your priorities

Getting started

Every journey begins with a single step. Before that first step is taken, you must make a conscious decision that you want to set out on the journey. You must commit to the journey. You must have a destination in mind. You must have set your own personal goals.

Set your priorities

Having established your goals you need to set your priorities. There are a number of factors that help set priorities:

- The importance of the task.
- The urgency of the task.
- The immediate benefit it will bring.
- The degree of difficulty.
- The extent to which the task restricts progress elsewhere.

Focus on your goals

Keep your goals in mind when setting your priorities. Always give priority to work that helps you move onwards towards your goals.

Pareto effect

In 1906 Vilfredo Pareto noticed that 80% of the land in Italy was owned by 20% of the people. He noticed also that this effect was common elsewhere. Later other people noticed that the effect could be applied to many activities, including the working environment.

People noticed that, for nearly all activities, 80 percent of the benefit comes from 20 percent of the effort. The converse is true. This means that 80% of our activity only yields 20% of the results.

You can take advantage of this effect. You can concentrate on the minority of activities that reap the most benefit. Everything else should be dropped, rescheduled, reduced, delegated or avoided.

Distinguish between urgent and important

- Important activities are those that contribute to your personal or professional goals.
- Urgent activities demand immediate attention.

Urgent activities are often linked with the achievement of someone else's goals. They are usually initiated by others. They are often the result of someone else's poor time management.

If a task has a high urgency and high importance then it is a critical task. It could be an unforeseen emergency or crisis. It must be scheduled first. This is why you need to reserve some contingency time in your schedule every day.

If a task has high importance, but low urgency then schedule it for a time when you can give it the attention it requires. Tasks of this nature will constitute your main workload. Important tasks contribute to your long term goals. Your important tasks should be scheduled for your most productive time slots. More routine tasks can be scheduled for when you are less productive. Examples include filing, responding to e-mails and other correspondence, returning phone calls and completing expenses forms.

If a task has high urgency, but low importance, look to delegate the task. This type of task usually comes as an interruption from someone else. The task will be important to them. It is their emergency or deadline that must be met. Let them know that you cannot help with the task. Point them in the right direction and let them get on with it. Many people make the mistake of concentrating on high urgency, low importance tasks. If a task has low importance you should not waste any time on it, regardless of the urgency.

If a task has low importance and low urgency, it is a distraction and can be either cancelled, ignored or delayed. Examples include junk mail, surfing the internet without a specific purpose, gossip, complaining and office politics.

Focus on the desired outcome

Always focus on the desired outcome when setting priorities. Know exactly what you want to achieve. Consider whether or not the completion of the activity will provide any benefit to you. If there is no benefit, then you should drop, delegate or delay the task.

Review your goals regularly

Having set your goals, you need to schedule time to review them periodically. Your goals should have a degree of flexibility. They should not be restrictive.

You may find that your longer term goals change with time. What was important to you when you were twenty will not necessarily have the same relevance when you are forty. The important thing is to review your short, medium and long terms goals regularly. Modify your plans on each occasion in order to reflect your changing priorities and experience.

Chapter 4. Take action

Every journey begins with a single step

Every journey begins with a single step. Unless you take that step you cannot embark on the journey. You will not change until you begin to take action.

Success depends on your actions

Success is achieved by taking action. It cannot be achieved by inactivity.

Be proactive not reactive

Learn to be proactive and set your own agenda. Control your own destiny. Do not be reactive. Do not let others dictate your actions. Work regularly on your highest priorities.

Recognise your situation for what it is and take action to change your circumstances. Initiate change in advance of anticipated circumstances. Recognise and correct negative trends or situations that are likely to have an adverse effect on performance.

Take initiative. Question how things are done. Propose a course of action and follow through on it.

Concentrate on what you can change

Your actions should be concentrated on what you can change. Stick to your circle of influence. If you can change something for the better, and it moves you towards your goals, then carry out the necessary action.

Ignore what you cannot change. That is someone else's concern, not yours. If you have no power or influence to change something then do not worry about it. Too many people focus on their area of concern. They worry about things that they cannot change.

This road leads to anger and frustration. Often we do not have the power to change what is perceived as the bigger issues. Do not dwell on these issues. Concentrate instead on what you can change.

This is why you should switch off outside distractions like television news. Reporters focus on the negative news which sells papers. Stories of death, war, destruction, calamity and starvation prevail. Do not carry excess baggage. It will only weigh you down.

Work towards your goals every day

Do something every day to work towards your goals. Maintain forwards momentum at all times. Even if you can only spend 30 minutes on working towards your goals, you should do it today. Utilise some of your time each and every day to prepare for a better tomorrow.

Chapter 5. Monitor your progress

Regularly monitor your progress against your goals. Take time each week to review what you have achieved. Record your achievements, the resources used and how long it took.

Review your progress

Consider the following issues:

- What went well?
- What did not go so well?
- What obstacles occurred to progress?
- What else can I do to stay on track?
- What help do I need?
- Do I need to develop any skills?

Set milestones along the way

The road to success is always under construction. It is a long and sometimes arduous journey. Do not simply have a starting point and a remote destination. Identify the milestones along the way. Share these milestones with your family and friends. Celebrate reaching each of them in turn. Rest and recuperate at each milestone. Take a welcome break before continuing on the journey.

Target to be early

Plan to complete tasks early. If you plan to be on time, any unscheduled delays will cause you to be late. More complicated tasks involve interruptions, delays or distractions. Any of these can cause you to miss your deadlines.

By planning to finish before the required time, you will create a cushion against unexpected delays. You will meet the required deadlines even if things go wrong.

For the same reason, always aim to arrive early for appointments.

Adjust your goals

Do not be afraid of adjusting your long and medium term goals as you grow and develop. Do not be concerned if you decide to drop a particular goal and substitute it with a different objective.

Learn from your experiences

If something works, repeat it next time. If something does not work, then drop it and try a different approach. Learn from your experiences.

Chapter 6. Overcome setbacks

Setbacks are inevitable

Setbacks at work, just as in any area of life, are inevitable. They are an integral part of the process. It is possible to minimise them, through thorough planning and preparation. However, it is not possible to eliminate them.

You will come up against setbacks in your work. You will meet minor setbacks regularly and major setbacks occasionally. The important thing is how you react to and deal with the setbacks you encounter.

People react differently

Different people can react in a wide variety of ways to the same set of circumstances. What might be a minor irritant to one person could be a major obstacle to another. The stimulus is the same, but the response is different. What differs is the nature of the individuals concerned.

The same set of circumstances promotes different reactions and behaviour in the individuals involved. This behaviour is driven by the thoughts and emotions of the different individuals. The thinking is different because they possess different beliefs, attitudes and rules. They attach different meanings to things. Their thinking has been conditioned by their own experiences in life. They have been influenced by other people and events to see the world in a certain way.

You are in control

It is not what happens to you that matters. It is how you respond. We all have the freedom to choose how we respond to setbacks. No one forces you to behave in a given manner. If you adapt a defeatist reaction, then it is yourself who sets this agenda. Understand that you are in control. It is your beliefs and attitudes that dictate your reactions. If your behaviour is wrong, you need to alter your thought process.

Understand the importance of failure

Treat failure as an intermittent step. It is an opportunity to learn. The most successful people in the world fail the most. They also learn the most from their mistakes. They know what not to try next time. They treat failure as simply a preparation step on the road to success. The more they fall down, the better they become at getting straight back up again.

When you attempt to do something, you open yourself up to the prospect of failure. You also have the possibility of winning. You cannot achieve anything without first trying. The person who never made a mistake, never made anything. The road to success is often paved with failure.

If you are to succeed in life, you must be willing to prevail. You must first have the desire to win. You then must believe in yourself. Finally you must have the will to continue when the odds are firmly stacked against you.

Do not take it personally

Do not equate failure with your self-worth. Failure is simply the outcome from a given action under a given set of circumstances. It is not the outcome you anticipated. It is not the outcome you desired. Nevertheless, it is simply an outcome. Treat it like the results of an experiment. The outcome was determined by the input and the circumstances. Either the input was wrong or the circumstances differed from what was expected. All you need to do is repeat the experiment, using a different input, or under different circumstances.

The result has nothing to do with your self-worth. It is simply a setback. It is an opportunity to learn and improve next time. There is nothing final about failure. It may have knocked you back temporarily, but there is always the opportunity to continue on the journey.

Strategies for dealing with failure

- Recognise failure as an inevitable part of the process.
- Do not take it personally.
- Learn from every failure.
- Make contingency plans.
- Remain positive.
- Set things in context.
- Accept constructive feedback and criticism.
- Seek guidance and advice.
- Alter your approach next time.
- Do not let failure limit your ambitions.

Remain positive

Maintain a positive attitude at all times. The following tactics will help:

- Keep the end result in mind.
- Separate what is important from what is irrelevant or a distraction.
- Reward yourself with incentives for reaching each milestone.
- Set performance goals, as well as outcome goals.
- Make your goals progressively more challenging.
- Be prepared for setbacks.
- Treat obstacles as stepping stones.
- Recognise failure as an opportunity to succeed next time.
- Keep contingency plans.
- Ask for help.
- Learn from your experiences.
- Look at ways of improving your skills.
- Vary your tasks to help maintain interest.
- Prepare to be a winner.

Positive thinking improves your well being

By maintaining a positive attitude you prevent negative, self-limiting doubts from placing constraints on what you can achieve. Positive thinking improves your well-being. It is good for your health. It reduces stress. It makes you more resilient. It helps you to attract others to your cause. By maintaining a positive outlook, your creativity will improve. You will be more likely to achieve your goals.

Don't let feelings drive your behaviour

Do not let your feelings drive your behaviour. If you wait until it feels right, you will achieve little in this life. If you wait until a customer is ready to say yes, you might wait forever. Be proactive. Let your behaviour drive your feelings.

Change your behaviour

We are often unaware of how our behaviour affects others and hampers our productivity. One way to overcome this is to ask close friends, family or colleagues for honest feedback on your behaviour. Ask about your strengths, but more importantly, ask about your weaknesses. Ask them where your behaviour most needs to improve. Listen to what they say. Be prepared to take action on it.

Listen to feedback

Listen to all feedback you get from your boss or other superiors at work. React in a positive manner. Welcome criticism. By offering criticism, others indicate exactly how you should improve your basic skills or behaviour. They are pointing out what is preventing you from progressing to the next level. If you want to be promoted, you should welcome all criticism with open arms and act on it. Make sure you clearly demonstrate later that you have learned the lesson and have developed and improved your behaviour.

Challenge that negative inner voice

How many times have you dreaded a situation or task, only to find out that it was not as daunting as you first thought? You then wonder why you were worried in the first place. Most of our fears and worries are completely unfounded. They are the figment of our own imaginations. They result from negative conditioning. They are the limits that we set on our own development. Challenge that negative inner voice that wants to prevent you from reaching your goals. Do not limit yourself in any way.

Chapter 7. Stay on Course

Stick to the path

Meeting your long term goals is not a sprint activity. It is more akin to a journey, with stop off points along the way. It involves consistency of approach. It entails maintaining pace. It requires small regular steps in the right direction.

It is important that you manage to stay on course. You will face setbacks and problems along the way. Everyone does. The important thing is how you react to these obstacles to progress. You may have to alter direction if you begin to stray from the path.

Motivation and will power are the two key weapons in your armoury when things get tough.

Motivation can be maintained by always keeping in mind your long term goals. Imagine what it will be like when you have succeeded in your goals. Think about all the gains.

Your will power is what helps to sustain you along the journey. Think about the intermediate gains. Just reach the next milestone. Just make a start on the next task. Think about the negative consequences if you give up now.

Do not be overwhelmed

Do not be overwhelmed by your workload. Recognise that many activities can be delegated or scheduled for later. Concentrate on what you have scheduled for today. If the workload is still too high, enlist help or consult your boss.

You are surrounded by the results of other people's goals

Take a look around you. Every man made product you can see is the result of someone else's goal. Someone else conceived, designed and developed that product. This made it possible for others to manufacture, store, ship and sell the product. All of our infrastructure, transport, buildings and engineering works are the end result of someone's goals.

Even our domestic and farm animals have been deliberately bred in the form we see them today. Many of the plants in our gardens and fields have also been cross bred.

None of this would have been possible, without someone else setting goals and striving to achieve them. Goal setting is an integral part of the human condition.

Nothing can prevent you from reaching your goals if you believe in yourself. Work to your own goals, not someone else's.

Value your journey

The destination is important. However the journey is more important still. With clear intermittent goals the journey becomes purposeful and rewarding. Life is all about the journey. You should value each and every day. It only comes once.

People who are happiest and most content are those who have learned to enjoy the journey as much as the destination.

Take time out to enjoy the little things. It does not mean that you have forgotten the bigger picture. You will return to your tasks refreshed and invigorated.

Keep the right company

If you wish to be successful then you need to surround yourself with the right people. This includes friends, family, business acquaintances and work colleagues. Share your journey with others. Build a network of support around you. Foster relationships. Share your vision with your closest friends.

Consider if you need to add anyone to your current network. Who is in the best position to help you move towards your goals? You should learn from the people around you. Get yourself a mentor and learn from his experiences.

Those around you need to be supportive of your goals. If you surround yourself with negative or pessimistic people they will only act to hold you back. Perhaps you need to drop some people from your network?

Accept the cost

To achieve your goals you will need to give up certain things. You will have to drop certain habits. You will need to get rid of negative activity. There is usually an opportunity cost. If you want to study more at home, you may have to watch less television. The secret is to substitute positive action in place of negative behaviour. Do not leave a void. Leaving a void concentrates your mind on the absent negative habit. Taking up a new activity helps to keep your mind occupied on positive factors.

Increase your awareness

The first step to achieving your goals is to increase your awareness of where you are right now. You need to be aware of your habits, behaviour, personality and values.

You need to understand your strengths and your weaknesses. In order to gain maturity you need to improve your level of self-knowledge.

Break old habits

You can only achieve more by changing your habits. If you keep repeating the same actions, you will get the same results.

If a habit does not contribute to your overall goals then you need to break it. Certain habits are counter- productive. They are addictive. They are destructive. Put these habits where they belong, in your past.

Disrupt your patterns

One way to break old habits is to disrupt your patterns of behaviour. Do things differently. Break the chain. Look at things from a different perspective. Talk to work colleagues and see how they tackle the same issues. Avoid getting into a rut.

Exercises to strengthen your will power

Try these little exercises regularly to help strengthen your will power.

- When you feel like postponing something, do it right away.
- When you feel like starting that easy task, begin the tough one instead.
- Try something new.
- When you don't want to do something, like walk the dog, go ahead and do it.
- When you really want to say something, keep it to yourself.
- Talk to the next stranger you meet.
- Only reward yourself once you have completed that outstanding chore.
- Substitute a bad habit once per day with a good habit. Read that book tonight instead of watching television.

Form positive habits

An easier way to overcome negative habits is to replace them with positive habits. Repeat the positive action each day until it eventually becomes habit forming. Research suggests that this takes 28 days. Mark off each day by colouring in a calendar box. Watch your chain grow. By focusing on forming a positive habit you will not be distracted by the need to drop a negative habit.

Keep a personal journal

A great way to track your progress and learn from your experiences is to keep a personal journal. Just log the key events at the end of each day, with a brief description of the issues and the participants. Write down your thoughts about each event. How did you react? What were your actions? Should you have behaved differently? What can you do to avoid the situation in future? How would you change your behaviour to deal with the issue in a more professional manner?

Review your journal regularly with the passage of time. Reflect on your actions and what you have learned. The experience you have gained will help you cope with unexpected situations.

Do not compare yourself with others

Do not set your worth on the ability or performance of others. Everyone is different. Everyone has their own talents.

If you can perform better than others in a given area, do not compare yourself to them. If you do this, you might tend to ease up. You should always compare yourself with your full potential. Break an activity down and look at your performance in all its different areas. If you can improve in just one aspect, your overall performance will improve.

No matter how good you are at a task, if you look hard enough you will find someone who is better. Constantly comparing yourself with others can lower your sense of self-worth.

You are an individual, with your own unique set of abilities. It is not your prowess in one particular area that is important. It is how you harness these talents to reach your goals.

It does not matter how well educated you are, or how many qualifications you have obtained. Results are all that matter. To achieve these results all you need are clear goals, a working plan and the determination to succeed. With the right approach, there is no limit to your potential. So if you must make comparisons, then concentrate on the difference between your current performance and your ultimate potential.

Do not let consequences determine your attitude

People who maintain a positive attitude tend to achieve more in life. They determine and set their attitude at the outset. They do not let circumstances, results or the mood of others, dictate their attitude.

The correct attitude helps us maintain focus. It enables us to stick to the tasks we have set for ourselves. If you maintain the right attitude it will encourage others to help you meet your goals. People are happy to help someone who displays a positive attitude. They tend to avoid anyone who is negative in outlook.

Focus on your strengths

Make a list of all the things that you are good at. Keep this list in a personal diary. Add to it as more ideas occur to you. Refer to this list often. It will help you to overcome any negative thoughts or emotions that creep into your mind. Replace these negative thoughts with positive affirmations of your strengths.

Recognise what you have achieved

When working on larger projects we tend to focus on what we need to do to complete the work. If you are faced with adversity, consider taking stock. Take a few minutes to look at what you have already achieved recently. Recognise your achievements. Now think about your past achievements and everything you have learned in the last few years.

Imagine the end product and the reactions this will bring. This will give you the motivation to continue.

Imagine your regrets

Imagine your regrets if you did not manage to get this project completed. Think about how you would have to adjust to that situation. This should give some additional motivation to proceed.

Consider a different working environment

When working on longer projects consider working or studying in different environments to add variety. A change of scenery often helps.

Alter tack

You may find yourself sailing against the wind and tide. You may be unable to make progress. If so, consider altering tack. Try a different approach. Tackle a different part of the problem. Consider switching to a different project and coming back to the problem later.

Challenge yourself

Challenge yourself to do better next time. Keep trying to beat your target each time.

The comfort zone

If you keep doing the same things you will keep getting the same results. The only way to get better results is to try something new.

Do not withdraw from a task because you have not got the experience. Always be prepared to embrace new challenges.

Many people value the familiar. They cling onto what they know and trust. They take comfort in their daily routine. They prefer to mix and converse with friends and family only. They only feel at ease in their own familiar environment. They stick to their comfort zone. They stick to the habits that they have developed.

Step outside your comfort zone

You must be prepared to step outside your comfort zone. The more you do this, the more you can stretch the boundaries of your comfort zone. If you do not do this the opposite occurs. Your comfort zone will shrink in on you. You will withdraw from more and more activities, due to fear and apprehension. You will not meet your potential. In order to be successful you must be prepared to step outside the confines of your comfort zone. Outside of your comfort zone, all things are possible.

Self-discipline

High performers tend to be self-disciplined. Discipline involves applying additional effort when you feel like quitting. It involves doing what you should, whether you want to or not. It involves doing what needs to be done, not just what you want to do.

Discipline involves sacrificing short term benefit for long term rewards. Discipline is what gives high achievers an edge over everyone else. People who have the greatest discipline also keep long term goals. The desire to reach these goals promotes intrinsic motivation. This helps them to overcome obstacles and setbacks. They continue onwards when many others turn back.

Promoting self-discipline

To help promote self-discipline:

- Plan ahead.
- Develop a routine.
- Prioritise and schedule your work.
- Use effective tools.
- Set time limits on tasks.
- Stick to your schedule.
- Break larger tasks down into smaller, more manageable tasks.
- Avoid distraction and interruptions.
- Become proactive rather than reactive.
- Make timely decisions.

Discipline is all in the mind

Discipline is in the mind. To achieve the required level of discipline to meet your goals, you must think in a certain manner. Discipline is all about desire. You must visualize your goals. You must see the benefits of success. You must value the rewards over the cost.

If you want to win a distance race, you need to be the last one to slow down. It's not about being the fastest. It's all about stamina and perseverance. The race is not won in the first ten yards. It is won by crossing the finishing line first.

People usually don't just fail. They give up. They quit. They throw in the towel. To experience success, you must persevere when all about you doubt your wisdom. When you feel like quitting, decide to try again. Success may be just around the corner.

The higher you set your goals, the bigger the rewards. However the obstacles also tend to be bigger. The bigger the obstacle, the more determined you must be. To overcome the obstacles, you must keep the rewards in mind.

Consistency, discipline, patience and a positive outlook are the elements that lead to success.

Climb up or slide back

Continue to climb up, or be prepared to slide back. You either climb towards your goals, or you slide back towards your starting point. Take some action each and every day to move towards your goals. No matter how small this action is, it will continue your momentum in the right direction. It will also help to reinforce the right habits. The best way to reinforce positive action is to repeat it until it becomes second nature.

Time spent on positive actions cannot be spent on negative habits. The more positive actions you take, the less time is spent on negative habits.

Anyone can free wheel down hill

Anyone can free wheel downhill when things go well. However it takes grit and determination in order to cycle uphill against the gradient. The steeper the hill gets, the greater the effort you will need to exert.

Keep to your commitments

Make sure you meet your commitments. If you promise to deliver by a certain date, then do so. Build a reputation for delivering on time. By not letting others down, you will find that they keep their commitments to you also.

Influence the people who matter

Some people concentrate too much on socialising with colleagues and friends. You should develop good working relationships. However, you do not need to spend excessive amounts of time socialising at work. Concentrate instead on influencing the people that matter. Those are the people who can determine your future. Focus on results. Become relevant to the agenda of those further up the organisational hierarchy.

Chapter 8. Time management tips

Time places demands on all of us

Modern society places greater demands on all of us. We often get
to the end of a hectic day and wonder just what we have achieved.
Where did the time go? Even though we have been busy all day
long, we have little to show for it. There is no end product. Time
is a resource that must be managed.

Most people do not plan and organize their time effectively. They
do not achieve as much as they could in the time available to
them. A common problem is that people try to do too much in the
limited time available.

Time management allows you to recognise time wasters. Time
wasters eat into your time without adding anything of value. Once
you recognise these time wasters it is not difficult to eliminate
them.

Poor time management leads to overload, anxiety, excess pressure
and increased stress levels. The longer the situation is allowed to
continue, the greater the risk of the adverse effects on health and
well being.

Managing your time will allow you to achieve a better work-life
balance. You will reduce your stress levels. You will be more
contented. You will have a general feeling that you are in control
of your destiny.

Time is money

As far as most companies are concerned, time is money. Anyone
who can save the company time is a valuable asset. Getting things
done more efficiently contributes directly to the bottom line. By
being efficient with your time, you will achieve your goals and
develop your career.
Employers expect workers to manage their time. They expect

them to organize their work so that important issues get priority and deadlines are met. In order to manage your time you should:

- Set clear goals.
- Prioritise short and medium term goals in agreement with your boss.
- Keep a list of outstanding tasks.
- Plan ahead.
- Use marginal time, such as time waiting on meetings, travelling, etc.
- Develop a routine.
- Plan and schedule your work.
- Be productive, not busy.
- Break old habits.
- Use tools such as a diary, wall planner, personal organizer and calendars.
- Keep one diary for all your plans, schedules, meetings and appointments.
- Keep a clock on your wall.
- Set time limits on tasks.
- Target to be early.
- Stick to your schedule.
- Break larger tasks down into smaller, more manageable tasks.
- Delegate as much work as possible.
- Re-route calls to avoid distraction and interruptions.
- Become proactive rather than reactive.
- Make timely decisions.
- Avoid procrastination.
- Categorise and file your e-mails and paperwork each day.
- Remove yourself from unwanted circulation lists.
- De-clutter you desk and office.
- Manage your boundaries.
- Manage meetings effectively.
- Bin irrelevant information.
- Record how you use your time in a diary
- Screen incoming calls.
- Use phone calls rather than meetings.
- Learn to say no.
- Challenge the processes and methods used. Streamline activities.

- Get rid of redundant or unnecessary paperwork and procedures.
- Leave an hour free at the end of each day to complete any urgent tasks.
- Schedule time to review progress and reflect on how to simplify things.

Chapter 9. Work more efficiently

The working week

Your average working week should take no longer than forty hours. If it takes you longer to get things done then there are two possible reasons. Either you are wasting your own time, or someone else is wasting it for you.

You may choose to work longer than forty hours, in order to achieve your goals sooner. However the additional time should be spent on working towards your goals.

Create an activity log

The first thing you must do is log how you spend your time. Before you can begin to control your time, you must first understand how you spend it. Only then can you recognise and deal with your own particular time wasters.

Begin by logging your daily tasks and how long it takes you to complete these activities. Log the time you begin and end each new task. Log any interruptions and how much time was spent on them. Keep this log for at least a week, or two, if possible.

Review your activity log

At the end of this period colour code the activities into the following groups.

- Important tasks.
- Non important tasks.
- Crisis or reactive tasks.
- Tasks that should have been delegated.
- Interruptions and dealing with requests.
- Delays.
- Meetings.
- Paperwork, reports.

- E-mails
- Phone calls.
- Communicating, instructing.
- Planning.
- Travelling.

Colour coding gives a visual indication of the relative time spent on each type of activity.

Consider the most important activities

If you could only keep three activities from this log, what would they be? Which are the three activities that add the most to your long term goals? Concentrate on carrying out these tasks in future. Spend as much time as possible working on these activities. Drop everything else if possible. Just delegate, outsource, or eliminate all other activities.

Delegate, outsource and eliminate unimportant tasks

Be honest with yourself. Do you spend the majority of your time reacting to the demands of others? How much of your work do you initiate yourself? How much is initiated by others? Do you waste time on tasks that should have been delegated? Do you set your own agenda? Look to see if:

- You complete the most important tasks when you are most productive.
- You complete lower energy tasks when you are less effective.
- You can concentrate on the important tasks that you initiate yourself.
- You can concentrate on tasks over which you have total control.
- You can eliminate unimportant activities..
- You can reduce the number of reactive tasks.
- You can reduce the number of interruptions.
- You can delegate tasks that are not part of your role.
- You can eliminate time wasters.
- You can reduce time spent in meetings.
- You can group similar activities together to avoid time wasted

starting and ending tasks.

Question how things are done

Always question how things are done. Just because something has always been done in a particular way, does not mean that this is the best way to do it. Look at all procedures, systems and processes in your working area. Question each and every one of them. Do they add value to the company, or do they simply add cost?

Look at every regular task that is carried out in your area. Also look at all reports in detail. Look at all the regular meetings that are held. Look at all the written procedures. Question why things are done in the way they are. Question how these things are done. Are they really necessary? Question the need for rules and regulations. Do they prolong inefficient work practices? Get rid of all clutter, all padding, all unnecessary tasks and activities. Keep all processes simple and lean.

Improve methods by thinking outside the box

Lateral thinking involves approaching problems from a different, often unconventional, perspective. It requires novel or creative thinking. It involves forgetting how things are currently done. The methodology involves considering the issue as an outsider would. Imagine that you have encountered the problem for the first time. With no prior knowledge or experience, would you tackle the problem with the current methodology? Or would you select an easier method?

Question the need for reports

Consider every report circulated by, or received by, your team:

- Do you need the report?
- Is there anyone on the circulation list who no longer needs the report?
- Can the report be simplified?
- Can the report be issued less often?

- Can the report be automated?

Keep abreast of technology

By using the guidelines in this book you will develop an efficient method of getting things done. However, better tools and methods are developed all the time. Look occasionally at the latest available tools. Check how your colleagues get things done. You may find improved methods of managing your time and activities.

Adapt a *get it right* first time mentality

Getting things right first time saves time and money. Having to repeat tasks and repair work is inefficient and costly. Improving the quality of your work will also improve your overall efficiency.

Look at priorities from a different perspective

Sometimes we are too close to a task or a problem. We need to step back and look at the bigger picture in order to regain some perspective.

One way to decide on priorities is to view them from a different perspective. Consider the following:

- How important would my boss view this task?
- How important will this task seem in two weeks time?

Reward yourself

Reward yourself for completing tasks on time.

Cut off activities at the point of diminishing returns.

It is important to review the amount of time spent on individual activities. The first half of the time we spend on any activity will reap the maximum reward. You will then pass a peak, followed by a sharp decline. As we get towards the end of the task we begin to see progressively less benefit. The marginal rate of return diminishes. We might start to get distracted and jump from one task to another.

An example would be gathering information on-line in order to give a presentation. After a given amount of time you will have gathered sufficient information to give a good presentation. If you continue to search on-line you will get some additional information. However 90% of the information you come across will be a duplication of what you have already gathered. The rate at which you discover new and useful information will have diminished significantly. It is time to cut off this activity and start the next process. This might be summarising the gathered information in presentation format.

Cut off each activity after you have reached the peak and switch to something new, where you can reap more benefit.

Recognise when you are most effective

Everyone has different time rhythms. They have a certain time of day when they feel most productive and energetic. For some people this is in the early morning. Make the most of your peak time by ensuring that there are no interruptions to your work. Make sure that you schedule high value work to be completed when you are most effective.

A lot of people have a certain time each day when they are on a low ebb, or ineffective. This may be just before the afternoon break. Utilise this time of the day for low energy work. This might include answering e-mails or returning phone calls.

Practice makes perfect

The best way to get better at something is to practise as much as possible. By cutting out unnecessary tasks, we can reduce the range of different tasks to complete. When we specialise in fewer tasks we automatically become more efficient in completing them. The secret to success in any field is to specialise and become better at the task than anyone else. Practice makes perfect. If you are the best at providing a service, then people will come to you to receive it.

Common time management mistakes

A good way of improving your productivity is to understand and avoid the common time management mistakes.

- Not keeping a to-do list.
- Not setting personal goals.
- Not prioritizing.
- Failure to manage distractions.
- Procrastination.
- Taking on too many commitments.
- Confusing being busy with being effective.
- Multitasking.
- Not taking breaks.
- Not scheduling tasks.

If you manage to avoid these common time management mistakes, you will be more productive and more content. You will also experience less stress.

Avoid Multitasking

It can take about 30 percent longer to complete a list of tasks when you multi-task, compared with completing the same list of tasks in sequence. The quality of the work can also suffer when you multi-task. The problem is that you do not focus on each individual task.

Focus on one task at a time. Devote all of your attention to that single task. Close off any applications that you do not need.

Never attempt to multi-task while talking to someone. This applies if the conversation is in person or on the phone. It is disrespectful. It will cause you to miss or misinterpret important details.

Exercise alternate tasking

Fully engage with each single task in isolation. Then move on to the next task on your list. By focusing all of your attention on each individual task in turn, you will be more efficient and productive.

Utilise your time to deliver results

Use your time wisely to deliver results. Do not simply carry out activities for the sake of being busy. Be particularly wary of repetitive activities. Are they really necessary? Do these activities move you towards one of your defined goals? If not, then look at ways of delegating the tasks to someone else.

Read quicker

- Learn to skim read material for the information you need.
- Check contents or index first.
- Read executive summaries.
- Read introductions and conclusions.
- Skip to the relevant content and then read this in detail.

Give false deadlines

One way to always hit your targets is to give other people false deadlines. To make sure that others do not let you down, you can ask them to complete the task sooner than you need it to be finished. Never let them know that you have employed this tactic. Otherwise they will relax their target completion time. Also they may do this in future, with tasks that have a correct target date assigned.

This is a tactic best employed with peers who are not under your direct supervision. You cannot command them to complete a task on time. They have their own priorities, which they will complete first. They may perceive themselves as being in direct competition with you, if you both report to the same boss. So if you need the task by Thursday, ask them to complete by Tuesday.

Follow up on requests

Give people timely reminders of outstanding work. If you have asked for a task to be completed on Wednesday, remind the person first thing Tuesday morning. Do not leave it any later as you will add to the feeling of pressure.

Be prepared to do that little bit extra

As well as working smarter, be prepared to work harder. It will set you apart from the herd. It will allow you to achieve even more. It will improve your chances of promotion.

Chapter 10. Build the right team

The key to success is to build the right team around you. If you delegate 90% of your activities, then it is important that you get the right calibre of employees to carry out these tasks. Surround yourself with the brightest minds. Get people with the right positive attitude. Hire expert help where you need it.

Communicate with your team

Your team need to understand the overall goals and objectives that you have set for them. They also need to understand what is important and what is not. This will help them to work effectively towards achieving these goals. Your team should have a common purpose, a shared vision and the same core values.

You must communicate regularly with your team. This helps to keep them on track. Find out and think about what interests each member of your team. Use this knowledge in your conversations with them. Build rapport. This improves their willingness to buy into your ideals.

Look after your team

Look after your team and they will go that extra mile for you. Treat everyone with respect. Treat others as you would like to be treated yourself. Even better, treat them as they would like to be treated. Understand your team. Get to know what makes each individual tick.

Try putting people at ease before you start issuing instructions. Thank them for their input. Congratulate them on their successes. Praise them in public.

Beware of setting minimum standards for your team

It has become fashionable for governments to set minimum standards in areas such as teaching and health care. We now have minimum standards for waiting lists, exam pass rates, how quickly we answer phones, etc.

The problem with minimum standards is that many people treat them as acceptable or even maximum standards. They are the limit of what needs to be achieved. Once reached it becomes acceptable to stop and concentrate on something else.

All of the management time and effort going into measuring and monitoring this single activity would be wiser spent looking at better methods of achieving results. Worse than this, management spends energy and resources manipulating figures to disguise the real situation. For example hospitals will drop you from the waiting list if you fail to re-register after a given time period. They know that many people will fail to do this. This way the waiting list has reduced and their performance has improved. Everyone is happy, except the person who matters most, the patient.

Is it not more important to train people to deal with customer phone calls correctly? Why waste time measuring, recording, monitoring and reporting on whether the operator picked up the receiver on the fifth ring rather than the seventh? If they are too slow responding, perhaps the company needs more operators. Perhaps they should provide more on-line help.

Do not limit your team by creating false minimum standards. Encourage them to use their own initiative. Ask them to find better ways of doing things. Let them surprise you with their achievements.

Gain commitment

Gain commitment from each member of your team, not compliance. If the whole team is committed to your goals you will achieve them quicker.

Let your team share

Let your team share in some of your decision making processes. Hold regular meetings to discuss team projects and methods of working. Ask for their input. They will understand the detail of the work more than you do. They will probably have discovered better ways of getting things done.

By allowing your team to share in the decision making processes you will raise morale and generate interest in the work.

Teach people to think for themselves

It is better to teach someone to fish for themselves than to always have to feed them. Let your team grow and take on more responsibility. Encourage them to think for themselves and devise their own solutions. If someone comes to you with a problem, send them back and ask them to come back tomorrow with a proposed solution.

Never tell, just ask

Be polite in giving instructions. Ask people if they would not mind doing a task, rather than issuing ultimatums. It makes a world of difference in how you are perceived.

Provide the right resources

Provide your team with the best possible resources. They should have the best telephone facilities, computer hardware and software that you can budget. They should also have good office furniture and materials, as well as the right rest and canteen facilities.

Less is more

Do not overload your people with too much information. Keep instructions simple and clear. Give a brief indication of the reasons, but do not over elaborate.

Make yourself available

Nothing is more demoralising than a boss who will not make himself available to answer queries, or sign off on work. Make sure that you schedule adequate time to carry out these functions. Let your team know exactly when this time slot is available. Let them know how they can contact you in emergencies.

Be consistent

Be consistent in how you behave. Your expectations should not vary according to your mood. They should also be consistent with the passage of time. Treat everyone in the same manner. Everyone must work to the same policies and procedures. Show no favouritism. Allow everyone the same opportunity to progress.

Motivate your team

Praise employees publicly for doing a good job. Encourage everyone to do their best. Make the job more rewarding. Give your team greater responsibility and control over the process. Set realistic targets with a degree of challenge. Avoid overloading your staff. Encourage your team to make suggestions. Act on these whenever possible. Listen to their concerns. Lead by example.

Reward and promote your high flyers

The only way to keep your best people is to reward and promote them. Pay them what they are worth, or be prepared to lose them.

Photograph and display team events

Take photographs of major team events. Display them along with any rewards or certificates in a prominent place. Show pride in the achievements of your team.

Provide performance feedback

A good way to maintain focus and get the best out of your people is to carry out regular staff appraisals. Most people dread giving and receiving staff appraisals. They go through the motions, get it over with as quick as possible, and give a sigh of relief that it is over for another year.

You should approach the task differently. Realise that appraisals are an opportunity to:

- Celebrate success.
- Reflect on progress.
- Focus on objectives.
- Steer someone in the right direction.

Set a time for the appraisal and do not postpone it for any reason. Nothing can be viewed as being more important than the scheduled appraisal. Avoid all interruptions during the appraisal meeting.

Spend some of the appraisal time going over the performance since the last appraisal. Give praise where it is due. Point out areas that can be improved. Ask the employee about his feelings and concerns. Then give definite goals and objectives to be achieved before the next review. Schedule time to meet and discuss progress. Identify any additional training that might be useful.

Chapter 11. Learn to say no

Dancing to someone else's tune

At work you will be asked to take on tasks, responsibilities and objectives that you would not otherwise accept for yourself. The secret is not to take on unimportant tasks. If a task does not contribute to your long term goals, then avoid taking it on if you possibly can.

Distinguish between beneficial and detrimental activities

Before you consider an activity you must decide on whether or not it is beneficial to your long term plans. Activities are never neutral. They are either beneficial or detrimental. If they are beneficial you should engage in them. If not, then look to avoid them. This applies even if the task is urgent. Negative activities, once repeated become detrimental to our long term well-being. They are the chains that bind us.

Consider the consequences of not doing the task

The only way to work efficiently is to concentrate on important tasks and drop lower value tasks.
The secret lies, not in what you choose to do. Success is much more closely related to what you choose *not* to do. If the consequences of not doing the task are minimal, then drop it. Never let the things that matter least interfere with doing the things that matter most.

If the consequences of dropping a task are irrelevant, then just drop it. Concentrate on important tasks. This is how you will make the necessary gains.

Only choose beneficial activities

Once you have learned to distinguish between beneficial and detrimental activities the next step is to only ever choose beneficial activities. This is the way to get what you want from life. Always keep the long term view in mind. Drop all negative activities and concentrate solely on positive activities. This will immediately accelerate progress towards your personal goals.

Drop negative activities

You must first learn to say no to yourself, before you say no to others. After all, you are the one who takes on the additional, irrelevant tasks. Learn to say no to jobs that are not yours.

Understand why you have taken on these tasks in the past. Most people hold on to non-essential activities for the following reasons:

- They don't take long.
- They don't take much thought.
- They are interesting.
- They are fun.
- They are easy to complete.
- They have become familiar.
- They are habit forming.
- The give a sense of instant reward.

Whatever the reason, if an activity does not form part of your goals, then it must be dropped.

Understand your role

Understand your role in the organisation. What exactly are your responsibilities? Look at your job description. Consider the requirements of the role. Discuss this with your boss. What are the expected outcomes? What is the net product that you produce? Look at how the job integrates with others. Now jot down all the activities that you should be carrying out to support your goals.

Consider what you are doing

Now think about how you spend your time. How many activities contribute to your goals? Have you got a plan? Do you know where you are going? How can you arrive at your destination without effective tools?

Know your destination. Understand what you want to achieve. Know how to get there. Start out on this journey. Do not be sidetracked. Do not retrace your steps. Understand your actions and the reason for them. Look for better ways of getting things done.

Do not over commit

Do not over commit yourself. Do not volunteer for additional work unless it moves you towards your goals. Do not get sidetracked on a project. Do not take on requests for work outside of your remit.

Retain control of your diary

Retain control of your diary. Don't let other people fill it up with commitments for you. If you have a secretary who keeps your diary, then give clear instructions on how it should be filled. Let it be known how much free time you need each day. Give guidelines on the type of meetings you are willing to attend.

Manage your boss

Think about your boss's management style. How does he prefer to get things done? Are his instructions clear? Does he alter direction often? Does he micromanage? Does he procrastinate? Is it difficult to get hold of him when you need authority to proceed? Does he make things more difficult than they should be?

Consider the following action:

- Agree overall targets and priorities.
- Agree on your level of authority.
- Agree on deadlines.
- Agree on core activities.

- Ask for clarification where needed.

Accept the way your boss is. You are unlikely to be able to change him. Concentrate instead on how you can help him succeed. Bring solutions to your boss, not problems.

Why you should *not* say yes to every request

By saying yes to every request you:

- Lose control of your time.
- Interfere with your priorities.
- Add unimportant tasks to your workload.
- Increase your stress levels.
- Diminish your perceived worth.
- Lose the respect of colleagues.
- Allow people to take advantage of you.
- Allow people to take you for granted.

Why some people find it difficult to say no

Some people find it difficult to say no. They want to be helpful if at all possible. They feel they owe it to others to help them out when they are under pressure. They do not want to be impolite or disrespectful. They do not want to offend anyone. They want to avoid upsetting or annoying colleagues. They want to be seen as contributing to the team, by putting team goals above their own personal goals.

When to say no

You should say no when:

- The task is not important.
- The task does not contribute to your goals.
- The task is not your job.
- You are too busy on other activities.
- Someone else can do it quicker and better.

Be assertive

Learn to be assertive. Assertive behaviour involves balancing the respect for yourself and others. It is not like aggressive behaviour, where the need to win outweighs the rights of others. It differs from passive behaviour, where you are subservient to the whims of others.

Remain in control by learning to say no. Set your boundaries. Do not let the act of helping others deduct from your own productivity. Do not make a rod for your own back. Value your time. Avoid passive, submissive behaviour. Do not be a doormat. Respect your needs equally to the needs of others. You have a right to say no on occasion.

Do not modify your behaviour due to pressure from others. Many people adapt a passive behaviour pattern when confronted with aggressive demands. You need to learn to remain calm, but assertive. Stand your ground.

Tips for remaining assertive

In order to remain assertive try some of the following tactics:

- Specify exactly what you want.
- Make your own decisions.
- Don't let others put you down.
- Accept that you are equal to others.
- Stand up for your rights, but don't violate the rights of others.
- Treat yourself and others with respect.
- Take responsibility for you own actions and decisions.
- Develop an internal sense of self-esteem.
- Be specific about your stance or position.
- Repeat your position as required.

Just say no

Judge whether a task will interfere with your immediate goals. Would it delay the completion of other tasks beyond their deadlines? If so, then decline the request. Do what is right for yourself. Be assertive, but not aggressive.

- Indicate a desire to be helpful.
- Say that you would not be able to give the work the attention it deserves.
- Then decline the work immediately.
- Give reasons for declining the work.
- Express regret, but do not apologise.
- Do not leave your decision open for debate.
- Offer an alternative like sharing the task, or double checking results.
- Suggest someone else who is better suited to complete the task on time.
- Show them how they could make a start on completing the task themselves.
- Thank the person for asking.

Do not give detailed reasons for declining the work, unless your immediate boss makes the request.

Declining requests from your boss

Your boss will delegate as much as possible. If you do your work well, he may tend to delegate more to you than to other subordinates.

The only way to decline requests from your boss is to let him know about all of your current commitments. Be honest. Point out that the new request will lead to overload and delayed results elsewhere. Then ask him to re-prioritise by delaying certain tasks, or to delegate the work to someone else. Keep the conversation rational and matter of fact. Your boss will respond likewise.

Common distractions at work

Distractions may be from your boss, your subordinates, colleagues, visitors or clients. The distraction may be in the form of a phone call, an e-mail or an unscheduled visit to your office or desk. You may even distract yourself with unimportant activity such as browsing the internet. Do not be sidetracked by distractions. Develop effective mechanisms for dealing with distractions.

Dealing with interruptions from others

Interruptions from others disrupt the flow of your work. They interfere with more important or urgent tasks. In order to reduce the frequency of these interruptions you should:

- Schedule visits for a certain time-slot each day or week.
- Book a meeting room to carry out important work free from disruptions.
- Let people know when you should not be interrupted.

Insulate yourself

Learn to insulate yourself from distractions from others. In order to gain control of your work schedule, you must minimize distractions and interruptions. Learn to reject:

- Trivial requests that co-workers attempt to off load.
- Someone else's emergencies.
- Unscheduled interruptions.
- Irrelevant distractions.
- Negative gossip and office politics.
- Trivial or routine tasks.
- Work where you will be duplicating someone else's efforts.
- Unnecessary double-checking. Let them check their own work.
- Your boss's whims. Get him to justify the relevance of the task.

Stop people coming to you for short term fixes. Get them to identify their own long term remedies.
Help others to manage their own time. They will no longer need to come to you with their emergencies.

Getting rid of unwanted visitors

If someone does enter your office when you are busy, try some of the following tactics.

- Tell them you have a tight deadline to complete.
- Ask them to call back at a suitable time.
- Stand up to discourage them from sitting.

Close that door

Keep a limited open door policy for problems and issues from your team. Keep it open when you do not mind interruptions. This will be when you work on less important or urgent tasks.

For instance, you could make an hour available from 2pm to 3pm each afternoon for queries. You could use this hour for dealing with e-mails, filing paperwork and returning calls if you have no requests from your staff or colleagues.

Then close your door when you do not want to be disturbed. Let your staff and colleagues know that an open door means it is all right to interrupt, while a closed door means that you do not want to be disturbed.

Group issues to discuss with each person

Do not contact a work colleague each time you have a simple request. Group all of the outstanding issues and include them in a single e-mail or phone call. Add the items to your to-do list until you have several that you can cover at the one time.

Meet someone in their office

If you need a short meeting with a colleague, arrange to meet in their office. You can terminate the meeting when you have covered the issues. Just stand up, thank them for their time and leave. This is easier than trying to get someone to leave your own office.

Distractions at home

If you do work from home on occasion, then consider how to avoid the following distractions:

- Turn down the television or radio. Better still, turn them off.
- Turn off the internet.
- Log out of social networks.
- Switch to answer phone service.

Chapter 12. Organize your working week

Plan ahead

Plan your week before it begins. Check your diary for appointments and events. Think about any preparation work you need to do for meetings and appointments. Schedule in the time required to carry out these tasks. This enables you to arrive well prepared.

Next you should schedule time to work on important issues that will contribute to your short and medium term goals.

Have an action plan for medium size projects. Plan to spend time each week on some aspect of the project.

Check your to-do list and plan in any other activities that you can complete this week.

Weekly commute

Consider ways of utilising the time spent on your weekly commute to and from work. If it takes 30 minutes to get to work, then that is 5 hours per week that could be utilised. Consider travelling by public transport. This will free you up to carry out some work related tasks. If public transport is not an option, then consider taking part in a car sharing pool. If you share the car with two others you only need to drive every third work day. This saves on the costs and frees you up to work on two out of every three journeys.

Weekly review

You need to reserve quality, uninterrupted time each week to review your progress. Consider the following:

- Did you meet all of your objectives?
- Did you get bogged down in an individual task? Why?

- Should you have delegated more tasks?
- Where there too many interruptions? How can you avoid these in future?
- Where there too many unforeseen emergencies? Could you have anticipated and planned for some of these?

Reserve quality thinking time each week

It is important to schedule free time with yourself each week. Schedule some quality thinking time. This time can be used to look at long term plans and goals. Write down your thoughts and plans. Jot down the next actions required to move you closer to achieving your goals. This allows you to be proactive, rather than reactive. It also enables you to organize the correct resources to be available when you need them. If you need the input of others, you can organize this in advance.

Eliminate unnecessary business travel

Travel consumes a lot of time. Question the need for business travel. Take advantage of technology. Consider using the phone, e-mails, text messaging, Skype or video conferencing, rather than travelling each time.

Make the most use of your business trip

If you must go on a business trip, then make the most use of your time. Leave an 'out of the office' message on your phone and e-mail account. This will help reduce the deluge of messages when you return to the office.

Leave the contact details of someone who can deal with emergencies and routine requests. They will take care of some of your workload while you are away.

Bring a portable office. This might include laptop, smart phone and tablet reading device. You can deal with correspondence and e-mail at airports or in taxis. Take an expenses form and fill in all your expenses while on your trip. This saves having to do it when you return to the office.

Driving

When driving to new areas, make sure that you use satellite navigation. This saves time getting to your destination. Use your CD player to listen to motivational or self-development recordings.

Take time to meditate

Allow some time each week to simply meditate and relax. This will help you recharge your batteries. Quite often new ideas and inspiration occur as a direct result of taking time out to meditate.

Chapter 13. Organize your working day

Identify a time each day when you will not be interrupted

Find a place and time where you can be alone each day, free from all noise and distractions. Switch off all of your gadgets. Allow yourself at least thirty minutes of this alone time each day. You need to be able to just sit, think and plan. Most people arrange this time for the beginning of the day. You can also carry out this activity at the end of the day to plan the following day's activities. By planning your activities daily you will reduce anxiety and stress.

Plan the work and work the plan

Plan your working day before it unfolds. Make your plan first thing in the morning, or better still, the evening before. The plan lets you anticipate how the day will transpire. It helps prevent you from being caught off guard.

- List the tasks.
- Assign the priorities.
- Carry out the plan.

Plans are of no use whatsoever unless we carry them through to completion. You will only reach your goals if you are prepared to take action.

Plan all activities

You should organize your working day in a way that is most effective. Each working day should contain the following activities:

- Planning the day.
- Prioritising the workload.
- Scheduling tasks and completing diary and planners.
- Dealing with correspondence.

- Meeting subordinates and colleagues.
- Delegating tasks.
- Completing tasks.
- Updating your boss.
- Reviewing the day's progress.
- Planning for tomorrow.

Use your first hour effectively

Use your first hour each day to:

- Check e-mails.
- Update your to-do list.
- File e-mails and correspondence.
- Schedule meetings.
- Delegate tasks.
- Start the important tasks.

Deciding on your daily activities

You need a set of criteria in order to decide what should be done today and what can wait until another day. Also you need to know when to schedule particular tasks in order to be most productive. Use the following criteria:

- Schedule overdue tasks first.
- Next schedule priority tasks.
- Group similar activities together, to reduce set up time.
- Schedule the tasks for the right time of day.
- Plan to make the best use of your available time.
- Schedule important tasks for times when you will not be interrupted.
- Schedule easier tasks for when you are less productive.
- Schedule tasks so that they can be accomplished in one sitting.
- Where possible, complete one task before beginning another.

Set a realistic daily schedule

- Allow about 20% more time than you think you will need for

each task.
- Allow free time for unexpected interruptions or emergency work.
- Understand what you can realistically achieve in a given time frame.
- Allow a contingency time slot for the end of each day.
- Schedule regular breaks into your working day.
- Do not overload your daily planner.
- Allow time for dealing with paperwork.

By setting realistic goals and meeting them, you achieve a sense of fulfilment. If you set unrealistic targets, you will just end up with a feeling of failure and disappointment.

Daily action list

Your daily action list helps you see what needs to be achieved today. It helps you focus on your immediate goals. You will find it easier to avoid distractions by keeping a daily action list. You can use it to show others that you are already committed to activities and cannot take on any additional workload. If you must interrupt your work to deal with an emergency, your action list helps you get straight back on track.

Use your action list to measure your progress throughout the day. At the end of the day, refer to your action list and determine how successful you were in achieving your goals.

Delegate

Decide what can be delegated today. Allow time to allocate this work to your staff. Allow time to review work that you have previously delegated.

Consider availability of resources

Consider the availability of resources when scheduling your daily activities. You may need the input of others for certain tasks. Taking this into consideration will help prevent delays in completing tasks.

Schedule important activities

You should schedule important activities when you are least likely to be interrupted. You can complete important tasks without interruption by:

- Getting to the office early.
- Blocking your phone or diverting calls.
- Using a spare office.
- Letting others know that you cannot be disturbed.

Take advantage of slack time

If you have occasional slack periods of time, utilise them wisely.

- Make short phone calls.
- Deal with e-mails.
- Read a report.
- File correspondence.
- Update your to-do list.

Review your plans daily

Take a few minutes every day to review your medium to long term plans.

Chapter 14. Time management tools

You cannot manage time itself

You cannot control or manage time itself. What you can control and manage is what you choose to do with the limited time available. It is how you use your allotted time that is important.

Time management is life management. It involves prioritising activities to meet your goals and reach your potential.

You cannot save time itself

You cannot save time itself. It cannot be saved up and reused later. When it's gone, it's gone. It cannot be brought back. You can, however, make better use of your time. You can get more out of the limited time available.

Time management tools

There is a clear choice today between paper and electronic time management tools. Time management tools include a diary, wall planner, personal organizer, automated reminders on computer calendars and contact lists. Electronic versions are available on phones, computers, laptops, notebooks and tablets.

Using time management tools allows you to record the tasks that you need to complete. This frees up your mind to think creatively.

It is acceptable to use a combination of paper and electronic tools. However, make sure that they do not duplicate functions. Do not operate on two calendars.

Yearly or wall planner

A wall planner will help you see the bigger picture. You can mark holiday schedules, project deadlines, sales promotions, audits, major customer visits, business trips, rotas, etc.

White board

Some people like to use whiteboards in their office as a reminder for:

- Appointments.
- Meetings.
- To-do items.

Other people use them to brainstorm ideas with their team.

Cue cards

Some people like to use cue cards when giving presentations. Other people like to display them in their office. They write daily targets on them or other inspirational quotes. The idea is to create a new cue card message each day to help keep them motivated and on track.

The monthly calendar

Use your monthly calendar to schedule meetings, appointments, activities and deadlines. Make sure that you schedule time to achieve important tasks. This time is not negotiable. While emergencies may cause you to reschedule these tasks, do not allow them to be cancelled. Make sure that you attend important events.

Refer to your monthly calendar each morning to get a quick view of your up-coming commitments. You may have to schedule some preparation work.

It does not matter whether you use a paper or electronic calendar. The important thing is that it is portable and can be taken with you at all times. This will make it convenient to schedule meetings and appointments.

An electronic calendar has the following advantages:

-You can access it through mobile devices.
-You can print paper copies if required.

The contact list

Keep a list where you store the names, addresses, e-mail and links for all of your business contacts.

Access the cloud

You can take advantage of the cloud to store important information that you want to access from multiple devices or different locations. This information might be contacts, goals, projects and documents. You can then synchronise and share documents, spreadsheets, images or presentations.

Keep a diary

Your diary is a scheduling and reminder tool.

- Update your diary at the beginning of each day.
- Keep a single diary for all your plans, schedules, meetings and appointments.
- Put recurring weekly and monthly tasks in your diary as a reminder.
- Put important jobs first in your diary.
- Plan about two thirds of your day. Leave the rest free for what comes up.
- Record enough detail so that you can understand its meaning at a later date.

Set reminders

Set automatic reminders before appointments. Most electronic calendars have a reminder function. They can also be synchronised with mobile devices and accessed remotely.

Consider using an organizer

An organizer is a central tool that might combine a calendar, diary, contact list, daily planner, to-do list and note taking area. Using an organizer can save carrying several tools around at the same time.

To-do list

Keep a to-do list where you write down all the outstanding tasks that must be completed. Prioritise these tasks based on urgency and importance. Rewrite the list in priority sequence. Score items off the list as they are completed. Against each item on the list mark who will do the task and how long it will take. Also mark the scheduled start time and the expected finish time. Transfer each separate item to your diary for that date.

If you encounter a new task that must be completed, then include it on your to-do list. You now have a reminder of the need to complete the task.

Advantages of using a to-do list

- A list focuses your mind on the important issues.
- It allows you to consider all the tasks collectively.
- It allows you to prioritise and schedule tasks.
- It helps ensure that you do not forget tasks.
- It helps you order your thoughts.
- You do not need to remember everything in your head.
- It saves time.
- It helps you avoid distractions.
- You can monitor your progress as you tick off completed tasks.
- It gives you a sense of control.
- It is a working record of what you have achieved.

Your list should contain everything you need to complete, including short term, medium term and long term activities.

People who do not use to-do lists often have post-it pieces of paper littered about their work station or office. The problem with this approach is that there is a lack of coordination and prioritisation.

The daily planner

Your daily planner can be used to record your daily appointments, today's action list and any other additional tasks. Without a daily planner you become vulnerable to interruptions and distractions. To update your daily planner:

- Copy scheduled commitments for today from your monthly planner into your daily planner.
- Copy priority items from your to-do list into today's daily planner, based on available time and resources.
- Copy unfinished items from yesterday's daily planner into today's planner.
- Copy any individual activities from longer term projects.
- Schedule any activities arriving from your e-mails and other correspondence.

Use templates or forms

Use standard templates for as many documents as possible.

- Standard letters.
- E-mail replies.
- Agenda forms.
- Minutes.
- Reports.

Evernote

Evernote is a web based application, which can be used to:

- Make notes.
- Construct to-do lists.

- Bookmark websites.
- Take photos.
- Record audio.
- Automatically save and synchronise data across platforms.

Dropnote

Dropnote is similar to Evernote. It has the advantage of providing 2GB free storage.

Google Calendar

Google calendar is a free on-line calendar. It is web based so you can access it anywhere and share it with others. You can colour code different tasks or appointments. You can integrate your calendar with other Google applications such as documents, spreadsheets, G-mail or Google Plus.

Utilise your computer

If you prefer to use a laptop at work, make sure that you get a docking station so that you can use a full size keyboard.

- Do not log out during the day. Put your computer in sleep mode.
- Purchase as good a specification model as possible to increase processing speed.
- Connect with cable such as ISDN line rather than wireless, for quicker download.
- Create templates for regular work and e-mails.
- Use coordinated software packages.
-Use macros and short cuts for frequent tasks.
- Add frequently accessed sites to your favourite list.
- Attach frequently used programs to your start up menu.
- Set your internet browser to open on the application you use most.
- Backup your data.
- Set automatic reminders.
- Use voice-recognition software rather than typing.
- Clean up your computer once per week. Delete temporary files

and cookies.
- Delete web browsing history regularly.

If your work continually involves looking at two applications at once, then get a second screen.

Keep up to date with technology

Keep up to date with automated labour and time saving devices and applications.

Chapter 15. De-clutter and create an effective work space

Defining clutter

Clutter is material that you do not immediately require, that takes up space in your working environment. Clutter is anything that is not used regularly. Clutter is anything that does not provide immediate benefit.

The clutter on your desk and in your office is a reflection of the clutter in your mind. Psychologically it will weigh you down. Clutter is a manifestation of your lack of control. It is an outward sign that you are disorganized. Clutter leads to disorder and confusion.

Keep your desk clear

Keep anything you use regularly within easy reach. Your desk should only contain your computer, your phone, your diary, essential stationery and anything else that you use constantly. Only keep paperwork that you are currently using on your desk.

Do not let paperwork build up on your desk. It will distract you. It will continually remind you of other tasks when you need to concentrate on the work at hand.

Do not generate paperwork

People often put something in writing to:

- Cover for themselves in case things go wrong.
- Take an opposing viewpoint.
- Score points.
- Impress the boss.
- Justify their position.

Resist the temptation to put everything in writing. You could ring and deal with the issue. Alternatively you could make a note to talk to the person about this issue the next time you meet them. You could save paperwork by writing a reply on the original paperwork and returning it to the sender.

Delegate someone to filter paperwork

Delegate someone to filter your incoming mail. Ask them to:

- Bin junk mail.
- Reply to standard requests for sales brochures, prices, discounts, etc.
- Pass on everything else to yourself.

Handle every memo just once

Deal with correspondence once and completely. Clear up all correspondence each day. This includes e-mails. Do not revisit the same message several times. Bin it, deal with it or file it.

Bin it

If you do not need it, bin it. Do not hold onto information or memos just in case you might need them again in the future. If it is not related to your job function you will not need it.

Deal with it

Read it. Respond if necessary. Complete or schedule any action arising from the memo. Delegate tasks to others, if at all possible.

File it

Only file material that you will later need. File material electronically rather than in a paper format if possible. It is much easier and quicker to access in this format.

- Use a system for filing. You can file by broad category first, then alphabetical or by date order, etc.

- File material daily.
- Include reminder details for future reference.
- Purge old material regularly, if no longer required.
- Every time you access a file, bin any contents that are no longer needed.

You must keep your filed material to a minimum. Otherwise it will be difficult to locate what you need. You will waste time searching for material each time you need to access it.

Tips for a tidy work place

Time spent searching for things, is time wasted.

- Tidy as you go.
- If you don't need it, bin it.
- If you need it later, file it.
- Organize your filing system.
- Distinguish between your needs and your wants.
- Have a place for everything and keep everything in its place.
- Question the need for every piece of paper.
- Allocate time each day to file paper and e-mails.
- Discourage others from producing unnecessary paperwork.
- Keep your desk clear.
- Regularly clear out your files.
- Don't photocopy anything unless you require a copy.
- Archive and label old material and files.

Consider if you need more time or less clutter

You can make more use of your time by reducing the tasks that you need to complete. One way of doing this is to de-clutter.

Chapter 16. Communicate effectively

Always communicate in a positive manner

Always communicate using positive words and ideas. It instils enthusiasm in others. It improves mood and morale.

Meeting and greeting

When you meet someone for the first time;

- Smile and say hello.
- Shake hands and give your name.
- Ask for their name if they don't give it.
- Say that you are pleased to meet them. Use their name when you say this.
- If you are along with someone and they meet and talk to their acquaintances, introduce yourself and ask their names.

Use questions to build relationships

Asking questions allows you to control the direction of a conversation. It also encourages the other person to divulge personal information. In this way you can build empathy. By showing interest in others, you gain their trust. You have a better chance of influencing their behaviour. They in turn will show interest in you. They will associate with your values and goals.

By asking questions, you can get your team members to think for themselves. This way they provide the answers, rather than you. This subtle difference ensures that ownership of the task remains with them.

Use eye contact

Use eye contact to demonstrate that you are listening to others. This helps build rapport.

Listen effectively

If someone broaches a topic with you it is usually of concern to them. Listen carefully to what is being aired. It may just be the introduction to something more important that concerns the individual. Pay attention and do not let your mind wander. People notice when you are not listening. Do not think about what you want to say next. This is obvious to others.

Listen for concerns

Pay attention to body language when people talk. What do you detect in their tone of voice? Think about why the person has brought up the topic. What is their interest or concern? Listen for the unspoken message. People usually look for encouragement or affirmation of their beliefs. By showing empathy you can connect with them on a personal level.

Listen for objections

Use questions to demonstrate interest in the topic and the person. It is important to listen when you ask questions. You must listen to what is being said. More important, you must listen to what is not being said. Then focus your questions on this area. There may be a problem or some resistance to change that the other person is worried about broaching with you. You can only deal with objections once you have brought them out into the open. If they remain hidden they may be an obstacle to progress. The best way to do this is to ask the person how they feel about the subject.

Do not interrupt

Wait until someone has finished their point before responding. Give it a couple of seconds. Often people pause to gather their thoughts before continuing with their point. If you do interrupt by mistake, apologise and let them continue.

Care about what is said. Even if the subject does not interest you, it is obviously of concern to them. Show empathy. That is the way to win hearts and minds.

Do not change the subject

Do not change the subject. This demonstrates a lack of interest and by implication a lack of care and respect for the individual concerned.

If someone speaks to your group, do not start a side conversation. This demonstrates a lack of respect.

People are more interested in themselves

If you listen to others you can gain more influence than by talking about your own hopes, dreams and aspirations. No one, except for your spouse, your family and closest friends, wants to hear about you. People are mainly interested in themselves.

Compliment people

Make a point of complimenting people. Offer a genuine compliment on their appearance, their views or their work. Do this every time you interact with someone. It works wonders.

Encourage people

If you detect signs of self-doubt or concern in others, always offer encouragement. This may just be the hope and inspiration they need to persevere. Encouragement lifts morale and increases productivity. If you show support for people in this way, they will respond in a similar manner when you need their help.

Remember special events

Remember peoples' birthdays, anniversaries and other special events. Send a card, or at least congratulate them in person.

Chapter 17. Communicating with e-mail and the phone

Advantage of e-mails

E-mails are an effective means of communication. The use of e-mails offers the following advantages:

- They are simple, quick, inexpensive, reliable and efficient to use.
- They provide a permanent record.
- They can be circulated to groups simultaneously.
- The message can be sent to different locations simultaneously.
- You can attach files, documents or images.

Disadvantage of e-mails

However the use of e-mails can have the following disadvantages:

- E-mail is a more impersonal medium than the phone.
- You cannot guarantee privacy.
- E-mail is not the right medium for insensitive or personal information.
- The message may be misinterpreted.
- E-mails are often used to score points against rivals.
- E-mails can be a distraction.

Constructing e-mails

Every e-mail you send creates an impression with the receiver. You need to leave the right impression. This will help influence others and improve your standing within the organisation. If you do not have time to construct an e-mail correctly, then do not send one. Wait until you can give it the attention it deserves.

When constructing e-mails:

- Specify a clear subject line.

- Update the subject line when responding, if the thread has changed.
- Include a friendly greeting and sign off.
- Spell people's names correctly.
- Think about your audience.
- Consider your intention.
- Use correct spelling, grammar and punctuation.
- Keep sentences and paragraphs short and specific.
- Use bullet points to separate different subjects.
- Be accurate, particularly with dates.
- Use attachments, rather than longer content.
- Compress attachments if the file size is large.
- Only copy those who need the information to cut down on responses.
- Specify whether you need a reply and the deadline.
- Be careful not to appear abrupt.
- Avoid jargon or acronyms.
- Be professional.
- Include alternative contact details in your signature file.
- Check your e-mail for errors before sending it.
- Do not construct an e-mail if you are angry or emotional.
- Blind copy multiple users if you want to keep contacts private.
- If you send an e-mail containing an error, send a second clarifying e-mail.

Responding to e-mails

If an e-mail needs a response, then respond within 24 hours. If you cannot give a detailed response within this time frame, send an acknowledgement. Indicate the reason for the delay and when you can provide the information.

Acknowledge confirmations for appointments. The other person may be waiting to book it into their diary.

If only the sender needs a response, do not copy the other people on the circulation list. Give a complete response to every point. This saves time and frustration for the recipient.

Read the e-mail once and respond to it immediately if possible.

Process your e-mails

Categorise and file your e-mails and paperwork. Clear up your in box every day.

- Switch off e-mail alerts. They cause distraction.
- Allocate specific time slots each day to handling all mail and correspondence.
- Prioritise and process your e-mail.
- Eliminate junk e-mail and spam.
- Unsubscribe from anything that does not contribute to your personal goals.
- Immediately discard messages you do not need.
- Get yourself removed from irrelevant circulations.
- Keep your in-box for today's messages only.
- Clean up the in-box every day by dealing with every e-mail received.
- Encourage your team and colleagues to send fewer e-mails.
- Do not respond unless it is essential.
- Keep all replies short and to the point.
- Set up folders and file as required.
- Filter e-mails.
- Use templates to save time.
- Automate mailing lists.
- Set up auto responder to discourage e-mails when you are away from the office.
- Do not print out your e-mails unless you really need them.

Manage your e-mails

E-mails can be the number one source of distraction. In order to work effectively you must learn to distinguish between important, urgent, non-important and non relevant e-mails.

Every e-mail can be classified as either non relevant, a 'reference' e-mail, or an 'action' e-mail.

Delete it

All non relevant e-mails should be deleted at once. About half of your received e-mails will fall into this category.

If you don't need to read or action an e-mail, delete it immediately. When in doubt, delete it. Do not file something that might be useful in the distant future. Delete it, forget it. You have more than enough priorities to be getting on with.

File it

A reference e-mail is one you want to keep for later reference. You should file attachments within your document files or file the e-mail itself in an appropriate e-mail folder. Do this the first time you read the e-mail.

Do it

An action e-mail is one that you will process in some way. The information is related to some task that you need to complete. If the task can be completed within a few minutes then do it immediately. About one third of your e-mails will fall into this action category.

Delegate it

Some e-mails need to be dealt with, but the action may take too long or may not contribute to your personal goals. In this case delegate the task. Forward it on to the appropriate person with a short note asking them to deal with it.

Defer the action

If the action will consume a significant amount of time, add the task to your to-do list. You can file the e-mail in a to-do section for later reference if required. Otherwise delete it.

Use the phone instead

The phone is a more personal medium. It should be used when building relationships. It allows you to gauge reaction, persuade others and get immediate feedback and responses.

The phone is a better medium if you want to:

- Arrange a meeting or appointment.
- Discuss the merits of different options.
- Agree on a proposed course of action.
- Persuade the other person to take a desired course of action.
- Respond to a negative e-mail.

However, most people spend longer on the phone than they need to by:

- Talking too long.
- Chatting about personal, unrelated issues.
- Not knowing how to terminate the conversation.
- Accepting all calls.
- Not screening calls.

Phone functionality

Use a phone that displays the call duration. Use speed dial keys. Take advantage of hands free options. Use conference call facilities to save travelling to meetings.

Making phone calls

- Plan and list topics for discussion in advance.
- Ask if the time is convenient to discuss the issue.
- Keep phone calls short and to the point.
- Learn to terminate a conversation.
- Summarise what has been agreed at the end of the conversation.

Receiving phone calls

Do not let phone calls interrupt your work. Only give your mobile or cell number to people that you want to have direct access to you. Everyone else should go through your company operator. This will help filter out unwanted calls.

- Use answer phone service, or re-route calls, to avoid distraction and interruptions.
- Arrange to call someone back if you are busy.
- Get the receptionist to screen your phone calls.
- Separate chat from business.

If you screen your calls, make sure you give guidelines on who should be allowed through, such as your boss.

Chapter 18. Influence others

Go straight to the decision maker

Go straight to the decision maker with your requests. Find out who the decision makers are in your organisation and with your customers and suppliers. Get their business cards. Get their personal mobile or cell numbers. Go straight to them when you need action. If you go through their subordinates or secretaries you will be delayed. The message will be filtered and relayed. So will the response. You will have to wait and put in twice the effort in order to get a response.

Use the preferred medium of the other person

Some people hate to use e-mail. You may have sent a customer several e-mails in the past, without a timely response. Yet, when you ring and leave a message, they get straight back to you. The assumption you should make is that they prefer to do all their business on the phone. If you want to do business with this customer, then the obvious thing to do is use the phone.

Other people never return their calls, but will respond to a text message.

If you want to be more effective in your communications, then use the preferred medium of the other person.

Talk about their favourite subject

When you do engage in small talk with others, make sure that you talk about their favourite subject. This is usually themselves, their children or their hobbies. Listen and ask follow up questions. Build rapport. The next time you speak to this person, return to their favourite topic. This shows that you have been listening. The fact that you have remembered, shows that you care about them as an individual.

When you move onto talking about business the other person will be more receptive. They will open up and give you more information. You will have a much better chance of sealing a deal, or agreeing a course of action.

If you show an interest in others and what is important to them, they will take an interest in you.

Speak their language

Speak to people on their own terms. Echo their views and their beliefs. Talk about what interests them. Relate to everyone in your workplace, regardless of their station. Take time to greet people and be polite to them.

Be positive in outlook

By remaining positive in outlook you will find it easier to attract others to your cause. Banish negative vocabulary from all of your conversations. It turns people off.

Identify win-win outcomes

Point out what others can gain from your proposals. It is the quickest and easiest way to gain their support. Most people want to know what is in it for them. They are not generally interested in your concerns. They have their own agenda. People either want to gain something from a proposal or they want to avoid losing something. Pitch your sale accordingly.

Be willing to compromise

If you can find a compromise it is often enough to seal a deal. So start out by asking for more than you need and then show some willingness to compromise.

Get to the point

People are busy and often preoccupied with their own concerns.

Get to the point quickly and explain exactly what you want.

Use peer pressure

You may want to win someone over to your viewpoint. If you have already signed some people up, then use this as a lever to get them on board.

Thank people

If someone shows you help and support, thank them in person and in writing. Be prepared to return a favour if it does not cost much. This will build up good will for any future interaction.

Express optimism and enthusiasm

Express optimism and enthusiasm for your ideas. This is often enough to get other people to want to be involved.

Look out for body language

Study the body language of others. Do not bring up requests if the time is not right. If someone is in a bad mood there is little point in trying to seek their support for your pet cause. They will not be receptive if they are preoccupied with other concerns.

Never tell someone that they are wrong

Never, ever, tell someone that they are wrong, even when it is obvious that they are. They will harbour resentment. Just suggest an alternative idea without passing comment on their viewpoint. If they are adamant about their belief, then drop the topic. You can work on what you want them to do another time, by using a different approach.

Let them think it was their idea

People will support a cause much more enthusiastically if they believe it was their idea in the first place. Sometimes you can prompt someone by raising the topic and asking for advice. They may well suggest the course of action that you originally had in mind. The difference now is that the idea is theirs. You can now ask for and enlist their help.

Help others first

If it does not take much effort, why not help others first? They are more likely to give you support on an issue that is more important to you.

Actions speak louder than words

People will judge you on your behaviour, rather than on what you profess to believe. Your actions need to backup your words.

Use facts and figures

Verify your ideas with facts and figures. Show that your proposals are consistent with studies, research or expert viewpoints. This adds a degree of legitimacy to your argument.

Sell yourself

Do something each day to sell your ideas, beliefs and passions. You must project enthusiasm for your role. Believe in your goals. This will help influence others to join you and help you get where you want to be.

Maintain integrity

Maintain integrity in everything you do. Set high standards of behaviour and professionalism in your dealings with others. Build a reputation for integrity. Integrity breeds trust and trust brings support and additional business.

Chapter 19. Overcome Procrastination

Recognise procrastination for what it is

Procrastination is a time thief. It steals your productivity. It impoverishes you. Procrastination involves putting off tasks that should be tackled sooner. When someone procrastinates they begin to feel guilty that they have not yet started the task. They dread starting the work and often fail to complete it on schedule. They are not clear where or how they should begin. They welcome interruptions as an excuse to avoid beginning the task.

Tasks that people avoid

People put off tasks that are:

- Boring.
- Complicated.
- Lacking deadlines.
- Awaiting additional input.
- Unpleasant.
- Awaiting a major decision.

Fear

Fear is a negative emotion. Negative emotions block the flow of potential. Fear stops people taking action. Fear holds people back. There are various underlying contributing factors:

- Fear of failure.
- Fear of taking risks.
- Fear of rejection.
- Fear of the unknown.
- Fear of success.
- Fear of public speaking
- Fear of changing jobs.
- Fear of speaking to senior managers.
- Fear on conveying negative news.

The problem with giving into fear

By giving in to fear you:

- Lower your self-esteem.
- Feel helpless and frustrated.
- Put obstacles in the way of achieving success.
- Fail to progress.

Control your fear

Think about things you used to fear, but have now overcome. Where is your fear now for riding a bike, or swimming, or driving a car? Remember that once confronted, fears tend to just disappear. It is just a matter of self-belief and self-confidence.

Learn to overcome your fears by applying the following steps:

- Identify and define exactly what it is that you fear.
- Evaluate the level of your fear.
- Identify the underlying concern or limiting belief.
- Challenge that limiting belief.
- Visualize the fear diminishing and receding.
- Think about the rewards when you overcome your fear.
- Talk about your fears and concerns with family and friends.
Listen to their words of encouragement.
- Take small risks first.
- Gradually increase the level of risk you are willing to take.
- Reward yourself for any progress.
- Have a backup plan of action. This reduces the fear of failure.

Apply reason

Ask yourself:

- Why am I putting off the task?
- What will be the impact of not completing the task?
- What is the worst thing that can happen if I take action?

- What is the best thing that can happen if I take action?
- How can I take the first step?
- Can I enlist help?

Embrace new experiences

Personal growth comes from new experiences. By taking on new tasks we challenge ourselves and develop as individuals. We move towards our full potential.

The only way to finish is to start

The only way to complete a task is to start it. The best way to complete it on time is to start it early. You cannot cross the finishing line until you have crossed the starting line. Do not ponder the task. Jump in and get started.

Concentrate on the first step

If the task is large and daunting, it can help to just concentrate on the first step. Work out what you need to do in order to get started and take that first step.

Be decisive

The more you delay in making a decision, the less time you have to follow through with productive activity. Once you have analysed a situation and considered the options and the likely outcomes, it is time to reach a decision. If you are in any doubt get advice from your boss. Then proceed without further delay.

The following tips can help:

- Analyse the problem.
- Consider the alternatives.
- Evaluate the risks involved.
- Carry out a cost-benefit analysis.
- Narrow the viable options.
- Base your decision on the overall benefits to the company.

- Consult with everyone involved.
- Listen to your instinct.
- Take advice from your boss.
- Review what worked in the past.
- Think about the consequences.
- Propose an optimum solution.
- Consider if you can reverse the action, if things do not turn out as expected.
- Make the decision.
- Implement the proposed solution.
- Review the situation in terms of the lessons learned from the experience.

Traits of good decision makers

People who tend to make decisions easily have the following characteristics:

- They focus on action, rather than analysis.
- They accept practical solutions, rather than waiting on perfect answers.
- They enlist the help of others and come to collective decisions.
- They take responsibility for their actions.

Take action now

The past is gone and cannot be retrieved. The future is not here yet. We can only plan for the future.

The only way to get things done efficiently is to focus on all the actions that you can carry out today. Today is your gift. Focus on what you can achieve each and every day to move you towards your goals.

Overcome procrastination

Try the following tips to overcome procrastination:

- Think about how you will feel when you have finished the task.

- Commit to the task.
- Delegate the task.
- Decide on a course of action.
- Do not wait for the right moment.
- Do it now.
- Do high priority tasks first.
- Break the task down into smaller steps.
- Complete each step separately.
- Reward yourself for each target you hit.
- Realise that you do not have to complete the whole task in one sitting.
- If you find the first task difficult, make a start on an easier task.

Break it down

Do not feel that you need to tackle the whole task at once. Sometimes we feel daunted and overwhelmed by the sheer scale of a problem or project. The best way to deal with this is to break the project down to manageable activities. Then tackle each separate task individually.

Schedule clear up time for difficult tasks

Reserve part of an afternoon each week to finish off uncompleted tasks, or tasks that you have been avoiding. This is your clear up time. If you have been avoiding a task, do not let it go past your clear up slot.

Keep a tray for each day of the week

If you get paper correspondence that involves more than a few minutes to deal with you can schedule it for a given day. Simply keep a stack of trays labelled Monday through to Friday and post each task to a given day. Clear up each tray on the day concerned. Nothing will remain longer than one week.

Do not wait for things to happen

Never wait for anything or anyone. You may delay, but time will not. Waiting is a complete waste of time. It is unproductive. If you must wait then do something productive while you wait. Check your e-mails on your phone, read your notes, or write a memo.

Do not wait for someone else to take the initiative. The best way to get something moving is to make a start, wherever you find the least resistance. Go ahead and take some action. Move on, move forward. Time waits for no man.

Chapter 20. Do not strive for perfection

Do not strive for perfection

Do not strive for perfection. Perfection comes at too high a price. If you need everything to be perfect before you sign it off, you will not meet your targets. You will never be satisfied with your results. Do not look for the perfect answer, look for the practical answer. Recognise the standard that is acceptable for the needs of the business. Do not continually refine your work.

Perfectionists often fail to delegate because they feel that others cannot do the work to their own high standards. They continually correct the work of others. They get stuck on details. They fear making mistakes. They are hard to please. They avoid tasks if they feel that they cannot give them the full attention they deserve.

Think about the end user's needs. How will they use this information? Chances are, they will skim through it and extract the data they need. So what is the point of perfection?

Your best is good enough

We all want to create high quality work. You should aim to do your best in each situation. No one can ask for more from you. When you have done your best move on and tackle the next task. Do not revisit the work.

- Focus on your overall goals.
- Distinguish between important and non important tasks.
- Set time limits and stick to them.
- Do not spend too much time on low priority work.
- Keep your eye on the big picture.
- Trust others to complete tasks.
- Do not confuse the quality of the work with your own self-worth.
- Do not get bogged down with detail.

- Seek help and the opinion of others.
- Submit your work when it has reached the standard requested by your boss.

Fear of failure

Many people fear failure. This is because they believe that everything should be perfect each and every time. This is an impossible task. It is not practical. It is not achievable. It becomes an obstacle to progress.

Parents and teachers can mistakenly install this need for achieving perfection in children. They are told to aim for 100% in examinations. They are lead to believe that anything less than this is not acceptable. This inevitably leads to difficulties in getting things done. The bar is set too high. The goal is unachievable. The result is procrastination and excuses for lack of action.

Avoid information overload

Know when to stop when you have done enough research to carry out a task or project. Gathering additional information just gives you more to accumulate, filter, summarise, prioritise and file.
Do not get lost in the detail.

Chapter 21. Learn to Delegate

Value your time

Never do anything that you can get someone else to do for you. Reserve your time exclusively to action core activities that move you closer to achieving your goals. Everything else is simply a distraction. Drop it or delegate it.

Knowing how to delegate improves a manager's performance. It frees them up from routine tasks to concentrate on medium and longer term strategy. It extends their capacity to manage.

Delegating work helps to develop staff as they take on greater responsibilities. To maximise your efficiency you should only carry out tasks that you cannot delegate.

Authority

Authority is the power to make decisions, issue commands and control the output of others.
Authority in any organisation increases the higher you progress through the ranks of management. Authority flows downwards from the top of the organisation. Authority can be delegated.

Responsibility

Responsibility is the obligation to carry out tasks assigned to you by a higher authority. You will be expected to do everything you can to complete the task on time and to the required standard. You will be given a degree of flexibility on how to achieve the end result. You cannot delegate the responsibility. However, you can delegate the task.

Accountability

Accountability means being answerable for the success or failure of a task. Accountability is where the finger of blame will point.

Accountability cannot be delegated.

Remember that you are still accountable and responsible for all the work you delegate.

How to delegate effectively

- Set the work priorities.
- Decide what to delegate.
- Prioritise the most urgent and important jobs to be carried out first.
- Delegate as much routine work as possible.
- Delegate according to ability.
- Where possible, assign one person per task.
- Brief the person by explaining the task.
- Explain the background reason for the task.
- Define the objectives.
- Explain how much authority they have to make decisions.
- Match this authority with the requirements to complete the task.
- Set deadlines and targets. Offer support and encourage them to succeed.
- Get a commitment of understanding, capability and willingness from the person involved.
- Provide adequate resources to complete the task.
- Let go. Do not interfere unnecessarily.
- Be flexible about how they choose to carry out the task.
- Leave subordinates to complete the details.
- Provide adequate guidance and supervision, but trust and support your team.
- Monitor and track progress. Check on the results at agreed intervals.
- Tolerate, but correct mistakes.
- Pay close attention to critical factors.
- Encourage your team to report problems or difficulties promptly.
- Encourage your team to seek advice if required.
- Gradually delegate more to subordinates in order to develop their capabilities.
- Evaluate the work and the results. Consider if it can be done

more efficiently in future.
- Thank, praise and reward your subordinates for a job well done.
- If the workload is excessive consult your boss to see if you can get additional help.

Recognise your limits

Understand that there is a limit to what you can achieve on your own. There are only so many hours in a day. In order to get more done, without overloading yourself, you must learn to delegate.

Reasons to delegate

- It reduces your personal workload.
- It increases the free time you have available.
- It increases your productivity.
- It enables you to get more things completed.
- It frees you up to take a longer term view of things.
- It gives you more time to plan and supervise.
- It allows you to concentrate on where your strengths lie.
- It allows you to concentrate on the important issues.
- It ensures that things get done on time.
- It develops the skills of your staff and builds their confidence.
- It motivates your staff.
- It increases the responsibility of others.
- It helps demonstrate trust and belief in your staff.
- It fosters collaboration and team spirit.
- It helps you assess the capabilities of your staff.
- The work can be done as well or better by your subordinates.
- It improves your work-life balance.
- It ensures that the work continues, even when you are not there.

What to delegate

- Anything you don't need to do yourself.
- Anything for which you are overqualified.
- Anything that someone else can do faster, cheaper or better.
- Routine or repetitive tasks.
- Time consuming tasks.

- Anything that will help to develop your staff.
- Interesting tasks that will help motivate your staff.
- Entire tasks that will give your subordinates a sense of achievement.
- Specialist tasks to the appropriate experts in your, or other, departments.

Things you should delegate that people tend not to

Many people are reluctant to delegate certain types of tasks. They find excuses to hang onto non core activities that do not contribute to their goals. They will not delegate:

- Important tasks.
- Tasks that they can do better than others.
- Tasks that they can do quicker than others.
- Short tasks.

When to delegate

- When your priorities have been established.
- When you are overloaded.
- When deadlines are looming.
- When subordinates do not have enough work to keep them occupied.
- When you want a different perspective on how a task can be completed.

When not to delegate

- When you have been personally instructed to complete the task.
- When the other person is already overloaded.
- When the other person does not have the skill or experience to complete the task to the desired standard.
- As a punishment.
- When you know that the task will fail from the outset.
- When the information is confidential.

Fear of delegating

Some people will not relinquish tasks because they:

- Lack confidence or trust in their subordinates.
- Fear that the task will not be completed correctly.
- Fear losing control.
- Fear that it will take too long to explain how to do the task.
- Take pride in doing the task themselves.
- Want to appear busy themselves.
- Are afraid to overload others.
- Do not want to be accused of dumping their unwanted tasks onto others.
- Do not want to repeat the task themselves.
- Want to remain indispensable.
- Fear that their subordinate will outshine them.
- They have no one immediately available to tackle the task.
- Fear that the person assigned the task will continually interrupt them for help.

All of these reasons are just excuses for holding onto the familiar. Quite often the fear of delegating the task is not the underlying issue. It is the fear of replacing it with something new and unfamiliar.

Symptoms of poor delegation

- Subordinates who are not fully utilised.
- Missed deadlines.
- Overloaded managers with no time to communicate with their staff.
- Underutilised staff lacking motivation.
- Lack of direction.
- Excessive turnover.
- The need to seek authority for routine decisions.
- Unnecessary interference in routine tasks.

Deciding to whom tasks should be delegated

Consider the strengths, skills and capabilities of your staff before deciding to delegate a task. You should pick the person who has the correct skill set to complete the task in the most efficient manner. Consider which of your staff possesses the following skills:

- Resilience and perseverance.
- Attention to detail.
- Ability to analyse complex data.
- Decision making skills.
- Ability to supervise others.
- Ability to plan.
- Ability to produce reports.
- Ability to give presentations.
- Ability to learn new tasks quickly.

Avoid delegating to someone simply because:

- They are the first person you encounter.
- They are more willing to accept new tasks.
- Someone else suggested delegating to them.
- They are your favourite subordinate.

Delegating different levels of authority

You have freedom in the level of authority you delegate with a task. This varies depending on the complexity of the task, the familiarity of the task and the experience level of the subordinate involved. Always consider the level of authority you need to delegate with each task.

Level 1. Do exactly as instructed.

At this level the problem is clearly defined. The task is specific. You instruct a subordinate on exactly what to do. Minimum authority is delegated. Clear instructions, rules and guidelines are issued. A clearly defined methodology is specified. You retain authority for all decision making. You might do this the first time you delegate a task to a subordinate.

Level 2. Research and report the issues.

At this level the problem is less clearly defined. Scope is provided to investigate the problem and report on the issues. You retain the authority for any decision making and further instructions. You might delegate this level of authority to someone who has already tackled similar problems.

Level 3. Research and make suggestions.

At this level you delegate more authority to investigate and suggest possible solutions. You ask your subordinate to suggest the optimum solution. However you want to be made aware of the detailed issues and his reasoning. You retain responsibility for the decision making and the direction of the project. You might delegate this level of authority to a trusted, experienced subordinate who is tackling an unfamiliar or complex task. You just want to make sure that they stay on track.

Level 4. Decide on the course of action and keep me informed

At this level you delegate almost complete control to your subordinate. You want them to get on with the task. You just need periodic updates on their progress to ensure that the project stays on schedule. You delegate this level of authority to someone with experience tackling a more complex problem with which they are familiar.

Level 5. Look after this problem. Decide what needs to be done.

At this level you delegate the task permanently to your subordinate. It is part of their duties. They are free to tackle it in whatever way they please. They can choose to delegate it themselves. Your only concern is that the task is completed on time and to specification. How they achieve this is their own prerogative.

Keep track of delegated tasks

Keep a log of all delegated tasks. Keep details of who the task was delegated to and the start and expected finish date. Keep this information in a journal for easy reference.

Do not micromanage

Once you have delegated tasks, learn to let go. Do not micromanage. Let your team get on with their work. Just let them know that you are available to discuss any problems they may encounter. Do not demoralise your staff by hampering their ingenuity and creativity. Give them freedom to express themselves. Do not constrain them unnecessarily. Keep the bigger picture in mind. Let your staff get on with the details. Let them make mistakes. They will learn and develop quicker.

Do not let your team delegate tasks back up to you

Beware of the danger of members of your team delegating tasks back up to you. They may complain that they cannot finish a task or that they do not have the time. If the work needs to be reallocated, then give it to another member of your team. Do not take it on yourself.

Be careful about suggestions from members of your team that involve you taking on extra duties. If there is merit in the idea, then let the person who suggested it take it on as a project.

Make sure that all members of your staff understand their respective roles. Let them know exactly what you expect them to do.

Develop your team

In order for your team to grow and develop you must nurture them by progressively increasing their level of authority. The more they develop, the more they will achieve. The more they achieve, the more you will achieve.

Chapter 22. Manage stress

People suffer from stress due to an adverse reaction to excessive pressures or other demands placed on them. Stress occurs when the level of pressure being placed on an individual exceeds their ability to cope. Stress can reduce an employee's effectiveness and lead to absence from work due to the effects on health. Different people are more susceptible to stress than others. Factors such as general health and well being, personality, emotional stability, self-belief, culture and background all influence how people react to stress.

Stress induces physiological change

Stress induces physiological change within our body. This helps us to cope with the situation. In the short term we may get an adrenaline rush and experience the fight or flight response. When the reason for the stress is removed, our bodies return to their normal state.

In the longer term the body responds to exposure to continuing high levels of stress by stimulating the nervous, endocrine, and immune systems. The effect can be detrimental to well being and health.

Causes of pressure in the workplace

Up to a given level, pressure motivates people and increases performance. However excessive pressure leads to stress. Some people can cope with greater levels of pressure than others without being subjected to stress. They have better coping mechanisms. Stress can be caused by a number of factors:

Stress induced by the working environment

- Excessive workload.
- Meeting tight deadlines.
- Poor working conditions.

- Lack of resources.
- Demotion.
- Job insecurity.
- Excessive noise.

Stress induced by others

- Difficult bosses.
- Conflict with colleagues, customers, clients or subordinates.
- Bullying or harassment.
- Conflicting demands.
- Poorly communicated changes.
- Lack of management support.
- Inequality of status and remuneration for similar roles.
- Poor instructions or direction leading to confusion over job responsibilities.

Stress induced by ourselves

- Seeking perfection.
- Unsatisfactory work-life balance.
- Perceived unfair treatment.
- Feeling undervalued.
- Feeling inadequate.

Major events in people's lives

- Bereavement.
- Marriage.
- Divorce.
- Birth of a child.
- Moving house.
- Ill health.
- Financial concerns.

We all have our own stress triggers. What causes excessive stress in one individual, may be no more than a minor irritant to another person.

Symptoms of stress

Stress manifests itself in a multitude of ways, depending on the individual affected. The effects can induce physical, emotional, behavioural or mental symptoms. All of these symptoms will have a detrimental effect on your work performance. They can also have long term effects on your general level of health, unless corrective action is taken.

Physical symptoms

- Tiredness.
- Lethargy.
- Headaches.
- Insomnia.
- Nervous tic.
- Illness.
- Digestive problems.

Mental symptoms

- Loss of concentration.
- A reduced attention span.
- Slower responses.
- Poor judgement.
- Excessive worry.
- Interruption to sleep patterns.

Behavioural symptoms

- Withdrawal.
- Apathy.
- Aggression.
- Emotional outbursts.
- Over reacting.
- Unpredictable or irrational behaviour.
- Cynicism.
- Loss of appetite or over eating.
- Excessive drinking or smoking.

- Poor performance.

Emotional symptoms

- Mood swings.
- Irritability.
- Depression.
- Frustration.
- Impatience.
- Anxiety.
- Bad temper.
- Nervous exhaustion.
- Panic attacks.
- Irrational fears.

Employers' responsibilities

Stress is counterproductive for employers. Efficiency drops when an employee's performance suffers due to stress. Stress is one of the most common reasons for lost hours at work due to sickness. 13 million work days are lost each year in the UK due to stress-related issues.

Employers can help reduce stress levels amongst employees by:

- Clarifying roles.
- Setting reasonable and achievable goals.
- Looking for the symptoms of stress in subordinates.
- Work study and work balancing exercises.
- Improving communications.
- Listening to the concerns of staff.
- Implementing anti-bullying policies.
- Providing flexible working arrangements.
- Providing access to suitable counselling.
- Providing adequate work breaks.

Managing your own stress levels at work

You must deal with excessive levels of stress before they have an adverse affect on your health and well-being. Do not deny stress. Do not ignore stress. Deal with it.

The secret to dealing with stress is not to analyse your feelings towards the stress. You need to remove the issues causing the stress.

- Think about the underlying cause.
- Think about what you can do to reduce the stress.
- Analyse why you react in a given way.
- Review your workload with your boss.
- Delegate what you can to subordinates.
- Manage your time effectively.
- Prioritise your work.
- Organize your workplace.
- Learn to say no.
- Make decisions promptly.
- Be realistic in your work targets and the standards required.
- Delay work that is not urgent.
- Stop worrying. Lighten up and laugh a little.
- Take proper, regular breaks away from the work station.

Establish and maintain a support network

- Talk to friends or colleagues about your concerns.
- Enlist the help of colleagues when overloaded.
- Get rid of destructive or non supportive relationships.
- Seek professional help if you need it.

Develop the correct work-life balance

Look after your health. Take proper rest.

- Do not work excessive hours.
- Do not take work home.
- Take regular physical exercise.
- Spend time relaxing with family and friends.
- Plan holidays in advance.

- Maintain a healthy, balanced diet.
- Reduce alcohol intake.
- Stop smoking.
- Meditate.
- Begin a hobby.

Remove major causes of stress

If something causes you stress, you need to deal with the situation. If you constantly worry about a situation, then it is time to tackle the problem. You may have ended up in this situation through making a wrong decision or lack of experience. Regardless of the cause, you need to extract yourself from the situation.

Admit to having made a bad decision. Pay whatever the cost is and put the situation behind you. Cut your losses. Get out now.

Deal with conflict immediately

Deal with sources of conflict immediately. Perhaps you have employed someone and come to regret it. If someone disrupts the rest of your team and holds back progress, you must deal with the situation. Clearly explain the expected behaviour and what is not acceptable. Perhaps you can turn this person around. If not then go through the disciplinary steps one at a time. This will either lead to you terminating their employment or them quitting for an easier time elsewhere. Either way, they cannot be allowed to jeopardise the efficiency of the whole team. If you do not deal with a situation like this, you may lose one or two good employees. They may be unwilling to continue working with this person.

Take control

Recognise what you can control and deal with it. Recognise what you cannot control and stop worrying about it. If you cannot change the outcome, then do not worry about it. Refer it to the correct authority. Then forget about it.

Chapter 23. Manage meetings

Parkinson's Law

Parkinson's Law states that the task will expand to fill the available time. Perhaps you set an hour aside for a certain meeting each day. On some occasions the business could be concluded in only 40 minutes. What happens? The participants continue to sit on and discuss irrelevant matters to fill the available time.

Recognise when tasks are nearing completion. Finish them up and move on to the next task.

The purpose of meetings

Meetings are an important management tool. Meetings can be held for some or all of the following purposes:

- Imparting information to the group.
- Exchanging ideas.
- Dealing with group issues.
- Making decisions based on collective input.
- Setting common goals.
- Reviewing projects.
- Updating everyone at once on important developments.
- Collecting information.
- Obtaining feedback.

Meetings are not a forum for talking. They are a venue for deciding on a course of action. They must have a clear objective. All participants must understand the objective at the outset.

Decide if a meeting is necessary

If the purpose of the meeting is simply to brief people, perhaps this could be done more effectively by other means.

Schedule your meeting in advance

Schedule your meeting well enough in advance to ensure that participants can attend. Schedule the time, location, duration and the participants. Pick a location where you can be free from interruptions. Make sure that the location is well lit, at the right temperature and has adequate seating and desk space.

Draft a clear agenda

Only include essential agenda items. Order the agenda. Put important items first. Set a time limit on each item. Allocate more time to important issues.

Invite the decision makers

Keep attendance numbers to the minimum necessary. Each person should have something to bring to the meeting and leave with something to do. Consider why you invite each person:

- Do they have the authority to sign off on decisions?
- Do they contribute expertise for technical issues?
- Are they responsible for the area under discussion?
- Have they got the resources to get the task completed?

Certain participants may only need to be present to cover certain agenda items. Schedule their attendance accordingly.

Issue supporting material in advance

Distribute the agenda and any supporting information in advance of the meeting. Make people aware of how they need to prepare for the meeting. Let people read it in their own time. Reserve your meeting time for discussion and decision-making.

Hold the meetings at the right time

If you hold meetings at the beginning of the day, people are more inclined to sit on and gossip. If they are held at the end of the day, people are anxious to finish up and get home.

Begin meetings on time

Begin your meetings on time. Do not wait for stragglers. You are in control. If someone arrives late, do not cover the issues again for their benefit. This hands control to them. If they are inconsiderate, selfish and unprofessional, then that is their problem, not yours. Their behaviour will be recognised for what it is. Do not waste your time and that of the other punctual participants, by pandering to the whims of these people.

Include short breaks for longer meetings

If holding a longer conference with several consecutive meetings, schedule breaks as appropriate. Provide refreshments.

Chair meetings effectively

Meetings should have a purpose. This purpose is to agree a plan of action for every item on the agenda. It is the chairman's responsibility to ensure that this happens. For some poorly run meetings the only decision that is made is when to hold the next meeting.

The chairman should:

- State the purpose of the meeting at the outset.
- Encourage input and interaction.
- Keep the meeting under control.
- Stick to the agenda and the objective.
- Prevent compulsive talkers from dominating the meeting.
- Keep people on track.
- Keep to the time limit.
- Seek clarification if necessary.
- Limit time spent talking on less important issues.
- Summarise progress.
- Reach decisions on every item. Seek agreement and ask for a vote if necessary.

- For each item in turn, summarise the decisions and actions.
- Resolve issues rather than delaying decisions until future meetings are held.
- Agree action points, accountability and deadlines.
- Wind the meeting up, by summarising the main points.
- Schedule the next meeting, so that everyone can confirm their attendance.

Stick to the agenda

Do not deviate from the agenda. If something is not on the agenda, do not introduce it or discuss it. If others bring it up, point out that it is a separate issue, for a different meeting. If the issue affects two or three of the participants, then let them remain behind later to discuss it. It should not take up the time of all the meeting participants.

Do not have a section at the end for any other business. This is an open invitation to have a general gossip. It encourages people to bring up their pet hates or personal gripes. It is often used to score points at other people's expense. If someone wants to bring up a point make them add it to the agenda in advance. This keeps input to reasonable and sensible issues.

Keep minutes

Have someone keep minutes. Make sure that there is an action point for every agenda item. This should specify what needs to be achieved, the target date for completion and the person responsible for the action. Make sure that you issue the minutes as soon as you can. This gives people enough time to action their points before the next meeting. Put the initials of the person responsible for any action beside each item. This will make it easier for them to identify items for which they are responsible.

Copy interested parties who may not have been present.

Chapter 24. Manage projects

Why you should take on major projects

Working on major products gives you a great chance to network with senior managers from across the organisation. It is a chance to meet and influence others. It is an opportunity to promote your ideas. People who take on major projects often make themselves indispensable because they know more about the workings of systems than anyone else. As everyone else tends to avoid project work, the fact that you have volunteered will get you noticed in the right places.

Project definition

A project will usually be a one-off event aimed at implementing change. There will be a start and projected end date. Participants and resources will have been reserved for the purpose. The objectives should be clearly defined, measurable and achievable. There should be a specific outcome.

Planning the project

A plan is required in order to ensure that:

- Everything is taken into account.
- Tasks can be completed in a logical sequence.
- Resources can be identified.
- Bottlenecks can be identified.
- Varying workload can be managed.

Initial preparation

At the outset it is important to obtain authority to:

- Agree the scope of the project.
- Set the overall objectives.
- Get financial commitment on the necessary resources.

- Define the roles and responsibilities of everyone concerned.
- Set regular progress review meetings.
- Agree a target date for completion.

Gather the team

Gather the team at the outset and explain the nature of the project, the main deadlines and the roles and responsibilities of team members.

Scheduling projects

- Break the project down into smaller tasks.
- Order the tasks according to priority and required sequencing.
- Estimate the time required for each task.
- Complete a Gantt chart.
- Enter the earliest and latest start and finish dates for each task.
- Assign the tasks to individuals or teams.
- Work out the resources required.
- Allow time for approval and sign off at the critical stages.
- Leave gaps for holidays.
- Allow for contingency delays.

Project management tools

A number of project management tools can be used to plan and monitor major projects. Use computer based systems if possible. The results are easier to modify. They are also easy to copy and issue to interested parties.

- Flow charts
- Process mapping
- Gantt charts.
- Histograms.
- Task analysis charts.
- Event scheduling tools.

Focus on results

Focus attention on results. Set milestones along the way. Hold regular team meetings to discuss progress. Make sure that you issue regular progress reports. Set performance standards. Monitor and control the time spent on each task, the cost, the progress and the quality of the work.

Identify the stakeholders

For larger projects there are often many stakeholders. Identify who these people are. Stakeholders are people who are directly affected by the project. They have influence and can help you at various stages of the project. Get to know the movers and shakers within your organisation through the management of your project.

Deal with project setbacks

Deal with any setbacks by following these steps:

- Identify exactly what went wrong.
- Isolate the cause.
- Identify how to rectify the problem.
- Identify any additional spending required.
- Agree changes with stakeholders.
- Alter the timing of the project.
- Document and record any changes.
- Instigate any procedures to prevent recurrence of the problem.
- Issue a revised plan.

Chapter 25. Take time out

Schedule regular breaks

Make sure that you schedule regular breaks each day. You cannot concentrate for prolonged periods without becoming fatigued. Even if you are working to a tight deadline, you will still be more effective if you take regular short breaks. Your brain needs time to rest and recharge.

Do not dismiss breaks as being a waste of time. Breaks provide valuable down-time to enable you to think objectively and work effectively. In an eight hour working day you should allow 30 minutes for lunch and 10 minutes each for a mid morning and mid afternoon break.

Do not take your break at your work station. Get up and go elsewhere to give yourself a complete break away from the task.

Schedule personal time

You should schedule personal time in the early mornings or evenings to relax and also to exercise. Plan at last one weekly treat, preferably with your family, like going to the cinema or your favourite restaurant. Take time each week to relax and recharge your batteries. You should have one major incentive each week to help keep you focused and motivated.

Vary the intensity of your tasks

Do not work on demanding tasks for long periods of time. If you spend 90 minutes on a demanding task, leave it and take a short break. Then complete a simple task before returning to the complicated task. Continue this cycle until you have completed the major task. By varying the intensity of the workload you will allow your mind to relax and avoid the build up of stress. You will also discover better ways of completing the task by taking these breaks away from it.

This method of working will help you to avoid burnout. Your workload will not seem like a continual slog. It will no longer be a marathon. Instead it will be like a series of sprints, each one followed by a period of rest and then a brisk walk.

Chapter 26. Get ready for promotion

Begin planning immediately

The day you start a new job should be the same day you start planning to get promoted. Always set your sights higher than where you are currently employed.

Do your own job well

The first stage to getting promoted is to do your own job better than anyone else has ever done it.
You must achieve and then surpass all targets the company has set for the job. You can do this by first of all setting your own targets higher than the company requirements. You can then apply all the lessons learned in this book.

Target the next level up

Target the next level up in the organisation as your three year goal. Now carry out all the activities that will move you towards this goal.

If you want to be promoted to the next level, first get a hold of the job description for that level. Also get the job or person specification if possible. Look at all the essential and desirable qualifications. Note the ones that you are lacking. Now work out a plan on how to attain them.

Obtain additional qualifications

Obtain whatever qualifications you need. Undertake any additional studies that will help advance your career. Consider learning a new language. Enhance your computer skills.

Volunteer for projects

Volunteer on committees such as Health and Safety or Quality

Circles. It will help get you approved for additional training and qualifications. It is also a great way to network with managers from other departments. They will be the decision makers, or at least be a sounding board when promotion decisions are made.

Work with your boss

Find out exactly what your boss expects from your current position. Work out a list of the short and medium term goals. Then achieve everything on the list. Update the list regularly with your boss. He will soon notice how quickly you can manage to get things done. He will begin to give you additional responsibilities. This will put you in line for promotion at some stage.

Build rapport with your boss

Make building rapport with your boss one of your highest priorities. Get to know his main interests and hobbies. Talk to him about the things in which he is interested. Become his friend and confidant. Support him with his goals.

Work with your boss's boss

Your immediate boss is not the person who is most likely to promote you. This might happen if he is promoted himself. However if you are to be promoted sooner, without waiting for your boss to move up, then it is more likely to be his boss who will make the decision. You may be promoted to the same level as your boss in another area of the organisation.

So make sure that any interaction at this level is professional. If your boss is away from the office you may get direct requests from his boss. If you are asked to get information make sure you provide it sooner than requested.

Recognise behavioural requirements

People behave in a different manner at different levels of an organisation. If you want to progress to the next level then you must behave in the appropriate manner. Study how people behave at this level and interact with them accordingly.

Keep confidential information to yourself

If you are made aware of confidential company information, make sure it stays private until after the firm makes any announcements. People who cannot keep confidential information will not be promoted to positions of authority where they would be privy to such information.

Avoid office gossip

Do not get involved in office gossip. People who get involved in negative gossip about their positions and their boss are never promoted. Others quote them to more senior staff. Do not be associated with these people. If you do, you will be tarred with the same brush.

Bring solutions not problems

Never bring a problem to your boss without suggesting a viable solution. Unless the office is on fire you do not have to report a problem immediately. You should be able to take at least ten minutes to think about the best way to tackle the issues involved. Managers get frustrated when confronted by problems that subordinates should be able to tackle themselves.

Show initiative

Companies value proactive employees who are able to initiate change in advance of anticipated circumstances. This saves the company time and money. Do not wait and react to events after they have occurred. Show some initiative by recognising and correcting negative trends or situations. Do more than the minimum required to get the job done.

Monitor progress in your area. Regularly look at results. Check on feedback from customers. Look for discrepancies. Question how things are done. If results trend in the wrong direction or anything looks out of place, consider the issues. Review the problem with interested parties. Look at all the suggestions and feedback. Propose a course of action and discuss it with your boss. Implement the solution.

Think like a manager

Start thinking about what is good for the company and not just yourself. Look and talk about cost saving measures, health and safety, quality, efficiency improvements, communication and other issues that are important to management. The more you talk the talk and walk the walk, the more people can envisage you in the role.

Contribute ideas

Get yourself on committees and focus groups and contribute ideas and suggestions. You will be measured by your contribution to the company. This includes the ideas and suggestions that you bring forward.

Consider moving elsewhere

If there is little room for promotion then consider moving elsewhere. The opportunity for promotion is often related to the nature and circumstances of the company involved. If a company is expanding, diversifying or moving into a new area, there are often more opportunities for rapid advancement. If you are getting nowhere in your current position, then target the right company. Send a speculative application if there are no advertised vacancies.

Network with other departments

Get yourself known in other departments. Opportunities will often arise in other areas of the company. Deal with requests from other departments promptly. Help people out and build your network of connections. Show an interest in how things get done in other areas. This type of information helps you see the bigger picture. It helps when answering questions for internal vacancies. Attend company events and use the opportunity to network with managers from other departments.

Apply for internal promotions

Keep an eye out for vacancies advertised on company notice boards. Apply for any jobs at the next level up, if you have the minimum specified qualifications. Look at the type of position that is advertised most often. If there are any qualifications that you are lacking, make sure you acquire them as soon as possible.

Get a mentor

Having mentor can open up a lot of doors for you within the company. A mentor can pass on a lot of useful information. He can point you in the right direction. He can suggest where you need to develop your skills. He can get you on committees. He can often authorise further training. He can promote your interests to other senior managers within the company who have vacancies in their area.

Groom a successor

If you become indispensable in your current position you may be chained to it. Make sure that you groom a successor. This will make it easier for the company to offer you a new position.

Suggest a new position for yourself

Create a new position for yourself. Suggest that the company should combine your existing position with responsibility for some other related area of the organisation. Give a rational reason for this proposal, such as cost savings by avoiding duplication

Develop a Positive Attitude

Success is more closely related to attitude than qualifications. If you are positive at all times and do not create difficulties for others, it is often enough to get you promoted.

People prefer to work around people who have a positive attitude. It is conducive to a stress free environment. If people like your personality they will be predisposed to helping you further your career. See the humour, even in difficult challenges, and help lighten the mood. People appreciate help and encouragement when they are struggling to cope. Be positive, cheerful and helpful whenever you can. It works wonders.

Dress to impress

Image is important if you want to further your career. Dress the part. Look the part.

Beat every target

Beat every target set for you. Deliver early on all of your promises. Be more productive than those around you.

Work to your potential

Apply the lessons in this book to work as close to your potential as possible. It is believed that the average person at work wastes about 50% of their time. Utilise your time fully and you will be twice as efficient as those around you. Concentrate on work that supports your main goals and you will be more efficient still.

Treat every assignment as a test

Treat every assignment you receive as a test of your capability. Deliver results quicker than expected.

Ask for it

If you want more pay or a promotion, then ask for it. If you are refused the request then ask what you will need to do to attain it.

Get a commitment from the company to consider your request if you get the additional experience and qualifications.

Consider a lateral move

If the pathway above is blocked consider a lateral move. This may be useful if your boss is blocking your career progression. Never stay in the same job for longer than three years unless you can add more responsibility to the role.

A lateral move gives you fresh impetus. It broadens your experience. It exposes you to a different boss, a new department and new colleagues. The route forward may be easier from the new location.

Keep a record of your successes

Keep a record of your achievements. You can use it when answering interview questions. These achievements should be in addition to your CV details. Keep a record of:

- The problems you encountered.
- The solutions you considered.
- The corrective actions you took.
- The quantifiable benefits that accrued.
- What you learned from the experience.
- How you can apply this experience in the new position.

Promote yourself

Send a monthly bulletin to your boss on what you have achieved. Contribute articles to magazines and periodicals on your area of speciality.

Be resilient and adaptive

Be prepared for setbacks. Be prepared to try different tactics. If at first you do not succeed, try, try and try again. Never, ever, give up. You will get there if you really believe in yourself.

Also by Terry Melaugh

Get That Job - The Ultimate Guide

http://amzn.com/B00BV74E4E

Leadership - The Ultimate Guide

http://www.amazon.co.uk/dp/B00CMR0VAI

Thank you for reading this book

If you have found this book to be helpful to you in any way, I would very much appreciate it if you could take a quick moment to leave a review on the Amazon website.

Your feedback will help me to continue writing self-help books in the future.